The Parents' Guide to
COLLEGE AND
UNIVERSITY

Also by Dr Catherine Dawson

A Practical Guide to Research Methods
*A user-friendly manual for mastering research techniques
and projects*

'All students should read this. I've completed the research for
my dissertation and it was much easier than I thought, thanks
to this book.' – Amazon reader review

Learning How to Study Again
*A practical guide to study skills for mature students
returning to education or distance learning*

A practical handbook which will be of use throughout your
studies – it provides advice and guidance on all aspects of
study, from improving writing skills to passing examinations,
and on how to cope with the extra physical and emotional
demands associated with being an adult learner.

Returning to Learning
A practical handbook for adults returning to education

'Has the capacity to make intending learners feel less
alone as they consider joining that rich, extensive, yet
often invisible community of adult learners. Catherine
Dawson's book offers a rich resource of ideas, experiences
and contacts.' – William Lewis, ALI Inspector, Talisman

howtobooks

Please send for a free copy of the latest catalogue:

How To Books
3 Newtec Place, Magdalen Road,
Oxford OX4 1RE, United Kingdom
email: info@howtobooks.co.uk
http://www.howtobooks.co.uk

The Parents' Guide to

COLLEGE AND UNIVERSITY

**ESSENTIAL INFORMATION FOR PARENTS ON ALL
ASPECTS OF FURTHER AND HIGHER EDUCATION**

Dr Catherine Dawson

howto**books**

Published by How To Books Ltd
3 Newtec Place, Magdalen Road
Oxford OX4 1RE. United Kingdom.
Tel: (01865) 793806. Fax: (01865) 248780.
email: info@howtobooks.co.uk
www.howtobooks.co.uk

British Library Cataloguing in Publication Data
A catalogue record for this book is available from the British
Library

Cover design by Baseline Arts Ltd, Oxford
Produced for How To Books by Deer Park Productions, Tavistock
Typeset by PDQ Typesetting, Newcastle-under-Lyme, Staffordshire
Printed and bound by Cromwell Press, Trowbridge, Wiltshire

NOTE: The material contained in this book is set out in good
faith for general guidance and no liability can be accepted
for loss or expense incurred as a result of relying in particular
circumstances on statements made in the book. The laws and
regulations are complex and liable to change, and readers should
check the current position with the relevant authorities before
making personal arrangements.

Contents

Preface

This book has been written for parents who would like their children to go on to college or university after they have finished their compulsory schooling.

The education system is constantly changing and evolving – as a parent you may find it hard to keep up with these changes, especially if you have never been to college or university yourself.

This books draws together all the important information concerning further and higher education in one easily accessible source. It covers issues such as financial support, the qualification system, student expenditure and the important aspects of student life and experiences.

Also included in the book are useful addresses and websites so that you can access all the information you require, from making applications to university to finding out how to obtain cheap computing equipment.

I have been a researcher and tutor working within further and higher education for over 17 years. The examples and quotations used in this book have been collected over the last five years during my research with students and parents.

It can be a worrying time when your child first starts college or university, but it is also an exciting and important part of their lives. As a parent you naturally want to help your child to make the right choices, and you want to try to help them with their studies and life away from home for the first time. This book offers practical, usable advice that will make the transition easier for both you and your child.

1

Understanding Educational Opportunities

When I conducted some research with parents whose children were thinking about going away to college or university, many of them said that they were confused about the education system.

Some parents, like Lynn in the example below, felt that the education system had changed so much since they were at school or college that it was difficult to know what was available for their children.

> When I was at school there were O Levels and A Levels, universities and polytechnics. The smart kids got all their O Levels and went to university. Some of the others went to the poly and some went to the local tech. It was quite straightforward. Now it's all changed. When my daughter said she wanted to do her course at the local college I thought, how can she – they don't do degree courses. I soon found out I was wrong.
>
> Lynn, 42

Other parents who had not been to college or university themselves felt that the system was confusing and overly complicated. This made it hard for them to understand what was available within the different sectors and to know what qualifications were required for each sector.

This chapter provides a description of the British education system, the courses available within each education sector and the types of overseas opportunities available to UK students.

KNOWING ABOUT FURTHER EDUCATION COLLEGES

'Further education' refers to any education which is undertaken after the compulsory school-leaving age. Broadly speaking there are six different types of learning provider offering further education:

- **General FE colleges** – these offer a wide range of courses to students of all ages. Courses can be during the day, during the evening, full-time, part-time, day release or block release. Qualifications can be academic or vocational.

- **Sixth form colleges** – these are designed for 16–19 year olds and tend to be attached to schools.

- **Tertiary or community colleges** – these tend to fall somewhere between the above two FE providers. They have a greater number of younger students, although they also cater for older students, offering a wide variety of academic and vocational qualifications.

- **Agricultural colleges** – although these used to concentrate on agricultural areas such as farming and horticulture, they now offer related courses in areas such as business and engineering.

- **Specialist colleges** – there a number of colleges throughout the country that specialise in offering further education in specific areas such as art and design, music or childcare.

♦ **Private companies or colleges** – there are a variety of private colleges and training providers throughout the UK which provide courses at further education level. Some of these may have charitable status.

CHOOSING A METHOD OF STUDY IN FURTHER EDUCATION

Your child can choose from a variety of study options if they wish to study at further education level. They can choose to study full-time, during the day, which would involve more than 16 hours a week of study. Or they may prefer to study part-time, which would involve less than 16 hours' study a week. This may be done during the day or during the evenings. Some students choose to study part-time and work part-time in paid employment.

Another option is to choose work-based learning which enables your child to gain new skills and qualifications while they are working. Through this type of apprentice-ship scheme your child would work with an employer for an agreed amount of hours a week and receive a wage. For the rest of the week they would attend classes at their local college.

Another option is to study a further education course by distance learning or e-learning. This type of study enables your child to work from home using a variety of learning materials and methods. It is useful for those people who find it difficult to leave the home or who don't want to study away from home.

CHOOSING A PLACE OF STUDY IN FURTHER EDUCATION

Your child can choose where to study at further education level. Some students prefer to leave school and study at a further education college as this may offer more freedom and better suit their needs. Others prefer, instead, to continue into the sixth form at school. This provides continuity and students often progress into the sixth form with friends and classmates.

If your child is aged 16–19 their tuition fees will be waived for most courses. If they choose to study at another further education college away from your home town they may also receive a grant to help with residential costs. However, you should check with your local Learning and Skills Council to make sure that they are eligible as residential grants may not be provided if the same course is available locally (see Chapter 4).

KNOWING ABOUT HIGHER EDUCATION INSTITUTIONS

'Higher education' refers to education carried out at a level higher than A Levels or the Level 3 qualification described in Chapter 2. It tends to be delivered in universities or colleges of higher education, although some further education colleges may offer higher education courses. Also, some people choose to study through distance learning.

At this present time there is talk of university mergers. However, in 2005, higher education institutions can be divided into ten categories:

1 The two old English universities of Oxford and Cambridge.

2 The older Scottish universities such as St Andrews.

3 The universities of London and Wales which are made up of a number of specialist institutions.

4 The 'modern' or 'civic' universities such as the University of Birmingham and the University of Sheffield. Some people refer to these universities as 'traditional' or 'redbrick' universities. They tend to be located in a variety of buildings spread around city and town centres.

5 The 'new' universities which were built in the 1960s, such as Kent and York. These tend to be campus universities located a couple of miles away from the city or town centre.

6 The universities with a technological background, such as Surrey and Loughborough. Some of these are campus universities, whereas others are located in city or town centres.

7 The Open University. This provides courses through distance learning and is the largest university in the UK with more than 200,000 students. Although most students are aged 25–44 students can enter the university at the age of 18. Most students study part-time and work in paid employment while they are studying. The Open University was established to be 'open' with no entry requirements.

8   The former polytechnics which were granted university status by the Further and Higher Education Act 1992. These have close links with business and industry.

9   The privately funded University of Buckingham.

10 Higher education colleges. Some of these colleges are seeking university status, whereas others will remain colleges of higher education. They offer degree courses that are of the same standard as university courses. The colleges tend to be smaller than universities and are particularly suited to those students who prefer a less crowded study environment.

CHOOSING A METHOD OF STUDY IN HIGHER EDUCATION

There are a number of different ways to study at higher education level. Your child can choose to study full-time or part-time. Most full-time degree courses are three years in length and most part-time courses are four to five years in length.

However, if your child chooses to study a subject that requires a specific type of training, the full-time course may last for four years. This is the case on teacher-training courses, where your child may be required to carry out a significant amount of teaching practice. Or your child might choose a sandwich course where they could take a year's placement in employment, either in the UK or abroad, as part of the course.

Some degree courses can be studied by distance learning – the Open University provides this type of learning opportunity and many Open University students study part-time while they are in paid employment. This can be a useful choice for students who want to work and earn a wage while they are studying.

CHOOSING A PLACE OF STUDY IN HIGHER EDUCATION

As the list above illustrates, there are a number of different learning providers that offer higher education courses. Your child may decide to study at a traditional university or perhaps at one of the 'new' universities that used to be a college or polytechnic.

They may also decide to study their first year of a degree course at a further education college, or by distance learning.

If your child is over 19 years old they could decide to study at an adult residential college. These colleges work closely with local universities, offering the first year of a degree course in a supportive environment for students who may be unsure about their ability to cope with university life and study. Once the first year has been completed, students move on to the second year at the local university.

STUDYING OVERSEAS

If your child is interested in studying overseas, there are a variety of schemes available. The schemes listed below offer the opportunity to study overseas as part of a recognised programme of study in the UK. This means that your child will gain all the advantages of overseas study without being away from the UK for more than a year.

- **ERASMUS** – this stands for **European Community Action Scheme for the Mobility of University Students**. It is the higher education part of the SOCRATES programme which was set up in 1995. Its mission is to enhance education through European co-operation and encourage institutions throughout the EU to recognise others' qualifications.

  Through this programme your child can spend between three and 12 months studying in another European country. Each year around 8,000 British students take up the Erasmus challenge and since the scheme started over one million students have taken part in the programme.

  Opportunities are available in a wide variety of subjects and your child can take part in the scheme at any time during their degree except during the first year. If your child is interested in Erasmus, they should find out which UK institutions offer an Erasmus option for their chosen course. They can do this by consulting the guide *Experience Erasmus – the UK Guide for students entering Higher Education* (details below).

- **International exchange programmes** – many universities take part in an exchange programme which can include universities from countries all around the world. These tend to be open to third year students who are chosen for these schemes on the basis of their academic achievements and their 'ambassadorial' qualities. The number of grants available and the amount of money provided will vary between institutions. Your child should contact the international office of their chosen university for more information.

◆ **Departmental exchanges** – within universities many departments run their own exchange programmes with similar departments in other universities around the world. Eligibility criteria will vary, but in general will be based upon academic record and subject relevance.

◆ **The Association of Commonwealth Universities** – this organisation offers a variety of scholarships, fellowships and bursaries for students who wish to study in another Commonwealth country. Eligibility criteria and funding amounts vary considerably between the different schemes and competition can be strong. More information can be obtained from www.acu.ac.uk.

◆ **The British Council** – this organisation provides support for study and project trips abroad for young people at school and college. Grants and bursaries are provided for some schemes, and free tuition and accommodation offered on other schemes. More information can be obtained from www.britishcouncil.org.

◆ **Connect Youth** – this organisation is based in the British Council in London and develops international programmes for young people and those who work with young people. It provides information and advice on youth exchange programmes, volunteer placements and study visits. More information can be obtained from www.connectyouthinternational.com.

◆ **International Association for the Exchange of Students for Technical Experience** – through this scheme full-time, undergraduate students studying science and engineering, agriculture, architecture and related fields can secure short-term vocational training abroad. Students must be aged 19–30 and need to apply in the autumn term for placements beginning the following summer. Placements are usually for two to three months. More information can be obtained from www.iaeste.org.uk.

◆ **University scholarships, fellowships, grants and awards** – throughout the world many universities offer funding to overseas students who wish to study at their institution. Funding levels and eligibility criteria vary according to the university, country and nature of the scheme. If your child wishes, they can study part or the whole of their course overseas through these schemes. Details of these schemes can be accessed through the International Education Financial Aid website: www.iefa.org.

USEFUL INFORMATION

Useful addresses

More information about Erasmus can be obtained from the international office of your child's university, or from the address below:

ERASMUS
R&D Building
University of Kent
Canterbury
Kent CT2 7PD

Tel: 01227 762712
Fax: 01227 762711
Email: info@erasmus.ac.uk
Website: www.erasmus.ac.uk

Useful websites

www.open.ac.uk
This is the website of the Open University.

www.lsc.gov.uk
This is the website of the Learning and Skills Council. More information about apprenticeships, work-based learning and vocational support programmes can be found on this site.

www.connexions-direct.com
This site provides access to advice on careers, work, finance, health and relationships for young people.

Useful publications

UNESCO publishes a guide called *Study Abroad* which offers information on courses and scholarships available to students who wish to study overseas. It is available from:

The Stationery Office
PO Box 29
St. Crispin's House
Duke Street
Norwich NR3 1GN
Tel: 0870 600 5522
Email: customer.services@tso.co.uk
www.tso.co.uk/bookshop

The guide *Experience Erasmus – the UK Guide for Students Entering Higher Education* is available from:

Careerscope Publications
12a Princess Way
Camberley
Surrey BU15 3SP
Tel: 01276 21188
Email: info@isco.org.uk
www.careerscope.info

Your child may find the following books useful:

Heap, B. (2004) *Choosing Your Degree Course and University* (9th edition). Trotman.
Boehm, K. and Lees-Spalding, J. (2005) *The Student Book* (27th edition). Trotman.

2

Understanding British Qualifications

If you are unfamiliar with the education system, British qualifications can appear overly-complicated and confusing, as Greg points out:

> Talk about confusing. My son told me he needed such and such credits for this, and such and such credits for that. What are these credits? What do they mean? How does it affect what he can and can't do at university? It's hard to find out this information without appearing dumb.
>
> Greg, 45

Other parents in my research felt that the system of qualifications had changed so much since they were at school that it was difficult to keep up with these changes. They wanted to help with their child's decision-making, but found it hard to offer advice when they were unsure of what qualifications were needed.

This chapter describes the qualifications that are available in each sector to give you a clearer picture of how they all fit together. Although it may appear a little confusing at first, as your child progresses with their studies you will find that you begin to understand more about the type of qualifications on offer.

FURTHER EDUCATION QUALIFICATIONS

In further education colleges and school sixth forms your child will be able to study for a variety of qualifications. These are listed below.

- **A levels and AS Levels** – these qualifications are for students who wish to continue with their academic studies after having completed their GCSEs. Your child will need to have passed four or five GCSEs to be accepted onto an A Level programme. There is an emphasis on theoretical study, even in practical subjects. Most young people study three or four AS subjects in the first year and three subjects in the second year.

  Progression from A Levels can be to higher education, employment or further training. When universities make decisions about who to admit, GCSE and A Level grades, along with other factors, are taken into account.

- **GCE in applied subjects** – these qualifications are restructured vocational A Levels which are available from September 2005. These courses provide the opportunity to mix theoretical and practical work with some work experience if required. GCEs are based on broad employment areas such as business, health and social care, ICT and engineering

  These qualifications can be studied full-time at school or college and can be combined with other qualifications such as A Levels or GCSEs. They can lead to higher education, employment, apprenticeships or further training.

◆ **Scottish National Qualifications** – these qualifications provide a broad range of options for progression from standard grade and are available at five different levels in Scotland:
  – access
  – intermediate 1
  – intermediate 2
  – higher
  – advanced higher.

Most National Qualifications are made up of a number of units (National Units) which are accumulated as the student progresses through their course. These units may be studied singly or combined with a programme of vocational study. Successful completion of a National Qualifications programme can provide entry to higher level study, employment or further training.

◆ **Scottish Vocational Qualifications (SVQs)** – these qualifications are awarded at five levels and provide the opportunity to work towards a qualification in a variety of occupations from junior positions to senior management level.

SVQs enable students to enter employment or move on to further training. Students studying for these qualifications will need to demonstrate that they have acquired the level of skill necessary for that specific task.

◆ **National Vocational Qualifications (NVQs)** – these qualifications are designed for people to gain recognised qualifications to do specific jobs. They are work-related, competence based vocational qualifications. A list of competencies in a particular occupation is drawn up and the students will need to demonstrate that they can meet the competence level required. Qualifications are achieved through assessment and training.

Most NVQs are studied by people in full-time employment, although some can be studied at college with off-site training. There are five different levels of NVQ which are equivalent to the following qualifications:

- NVQ level 1 = GCSE D/E grades
- NVQ level 2 = GCSE C grade
- NVQ level 3 = A Level
- NVQ level 4 = degree/HND
- NVQ level 5 = postgraduate diploma/degree or professional qualification

◆ **General National Vocational Qualification** – this qualification is due to be phased out by 2007 so it may no longer be offered by some schools and colleges. At present it is designed for those wanting to study a broad area of work, with a combination of theoretical and practical study.

◆ **International Baccalaureate (IB)** – this qualification was taken by children who lived overseas with their families. However, some colleges are now adopting it in the UK. The qualification is recognised internationally and it is broadly equivalent to three A Levels. Most universities accept the Baccalaureate as an entry qualification.

The IB is designed for students who have strengths in a wide range of subjects, with the emphasis placed on critical thinking and intercultural understanding. Six subjects are taken together with core elements such as the theory of knowledge and extended essay work.

◆ **City and Guilds Qualifications** – City and Guilds provide vocational awards in over 400 work-related areas. They are designed to recognise skills used in the workplace and prove a person has practical skills in addition to theoretical knowledge.

City and Guilds qualifications are available at a number of different levels in many occupations, ranging from catering to plumbing. They are a useful qualification if your child knows what work they want to do and wants to gain qualifications specifically for that type of job.

◆ **BTEC** – this is a nationally recognised examining body which specialises in courses linked to commerce and industry. BTEC courses are suitable, in particular, if your child has a good idea of their future career. BTEC National Diplomas, Advanced Diplomas and National Certificates are available in a variety of subjects ranging from construction to sports and exercise science.

◆ **OCR Nationals** – these qualifications are designed for students who wish to develop their skills through work-related study. Students are able to begin with a general vocational preparation before moving on to a specific area of work. They can study either full-time or part-time at a further education college. OCRs are offered at three levels:
– National Award (Level 1)
– National Certificate (Level 2)
– National Diploma (Level 3).

HIGHER EDUCATION QUALIFICATIONS

In universities and colleges of higher education your child will be able to study for a variety of qualifications. These are listed below.

◆ **First degrees** – most higher education courses lead to a first degree. This could be a Bachelor of Arts (BA), a Bachelor of Science (BSc), a Bachelor of Education (BEd) or a Bachelor of Music (BMus). Most first degree courses tend to run over three years for full-time study, although some full-time degree courses may run over four years, with one year for work or study placement. Degrees can be taken part-time and may run for around five years. Some degrees are academic in nature, such as those in history or sociology, whereas others are more vocationally orientated, such as those in education or engineering.

In many higher education institutions subjects are now studied in *modules*. This means that your child can study a variety of modules which make up their degree. In a standard year, for most universities, they would need to complete 120 credits by studying a selection of modules, each worth anything from ten credits upwards. Some institutions, however, tend to follow a more traditional, single subject course of study, or specify the amount and type of modules that can be taken together. University prospectuses will contain details of the modular system.

Although the government is considering changes to the degree classification system, at present first degrees tend to be classified in the following way:

– 1st (over 70% in exams and coursework)
– 2:1 (60–69%)
– 2:2 (50–59%)
– 3rd (40–49%)
– Fail (less than 40% in course work and exams).

◆ **Higher National Diploma (HND)** – these tend to be studied full-time over two years and are advanced, vocational courses that relate to a particular occupation or field. HNDs are a useful qualification if your child knows what they want to do for a career. They are also useful for those people who are not sure whether they wish to commit to a full degree, or for those who want a gentle introduction to their studies. Upon successful completion of an HND students can enter a degree course in the second or, perhaps, third year.

◆ **Higher National Certificate (HNC)** – these tend to be studied part-time over two years. Again, it is a useful qualification for those who do not wish to commit to degree study. It is also a useful qualification for people who wish to remain in paid employment while they study. Upon successful completion of an HNC students can enter the second year of a degree course.

◆ **Foundation Degree** – these are employment-related, two-year courses, although it is possible to study part-time over a longer period. It is hoped that Foundation Degrees will provide an alternative route into higher education. Some Foundation Degrees are offered by colleges of further education in partnership with a university. Upon successful completion students can move on to an undergraduate degree course if they wish.

◆ **Diploma/Certificate of Higher Education** – these qualifications are offered by many higher education institutions. The certificate is generally studied over one year full-time and the diploma usually takes two years of full-time study, although both can be studied part-time.

Following the completion of a diploma or certificate in higher education, students gain credits which can be built up towards a degree course at a later stage. These qualifications tend to be offered in areas such as nursing and social work.

POSTGRADUATE QUALIFICATIONS

If your child wishes to continue with their education after they have completed their first degree, there are a variety of qualifications available. These are listed below.

◆ **Postgraduate Certificates and Diplomas** – these are studied over one year full-time, two years part-time or through distance learning. The qualifications are available in a wide range of subjects and tend to be vocationally orientated. The certificate is at a lower level than the diploma. These qualifications are available as stand alone courses or can be part of a Master's course.

◆ **Postgraduate Certificate in Education (PGCEs)** – these are available for people with a first degree who want to go into teaching. The courses are generally either one year full-time or two years part-time and students are required to carry out a good deal of classroom practice during their course. Some students who wish to become teachers decide to take this route as it allows them to study for a general degree first before training to become a teacher.

◆ **Master's Degree** – these degrees tend to be studied by people who have already received a first degree, although adults who are able to demonstrate a suitable level of work experience and competence may be admitted to a course without a first degree.

Master's Degrees are taught for either at least one year full-time or two years part-time, although some institutions will offer the courses through distance learning. Some Master's courses are not taught courses but are *research* courses which mean that a student undertakes a piece of research, usually over two years. Funding is available for Master's courses, but your child would have to obtain a good degree to stand a chance of receiving a studentship.

◆ **Master of Business Administration (MBA)** – this is a qualification for anybody interested in management and business. People who are able to demonstrate the required level of experience and competence will be accepted onto a course without a first degree.

Courses can be studied full-time over one year, part-time over two years or through distance learning. Part-time courses are becoming increasingly popular as people can combine the course with employment.

◆ **Doctor of Philosophy** – studying for a postgraduate doctorate involves in-depth research into a specific topic, decided upon by the student or institution. Your child will need a good first degree or a Master's Degree to be accepted on to a doctorate programme.

A student may conduct the research over a three or four-year period full-time or over four to five years part-time, although some people take much longer to obtain their doctorate. If your child is interested in studying for a doctorate it is useful for them to build up a good working relationship with staff at their university and they will need to obtain a good undergraduate degree.

◆ **New Route PhD** – using this route a student can study for a doctorate over a four year period and combine a specific research project with a coherent programme of formal course work and professional skills development.

USEFUL INFORMATION

Useful addresses

More information about qualifications in England can be obtained from:
The Qualifications and Curriculum Authority
83 Piccadilly
London W1J 8QA
Tel: 020 7509 5555
Email: info@qca.org.uk

More information about qualifications in Scotland can be obtained from:
The Scottish Qualifications Authority
24 Douglas Street
Glasgow G2 7NQ
Tel: 0845 279 1000
Email: customer@sqa.org.uk

More information about qualifications in Wales can be obtained from:
The Qualifications, Curriculum and Assessment Authority for Wales
Castle Buildings
Womanby Street
Cardiff CF10 1SX
Tel: 029 2037 5400
Email: info@accac.org.uk

More information about qualifications in Northern Ireland can be obtained from:
Council for the Curriculum, Examinations and Assessment
29 Clarendon Road
Clarendon Dock
Belfast BT1 3BG
Tel: 028 9026 1200
Email: info@ccea.org.uk

Useful websites

www.city-and-guilds.co.uk
This website provides more information about City and Guilds qualifications.

www.ocr.org.uk
This website describes the OCR national qualifications and enables your child to search for qualifications in your area. It also describes the assessment process in detail.

www.edexcel.org.uk
This is the website of Edexcel, an awarding body in the UK. The website contains details of BTEC qualifications.

www.ibo.org
Consult this website for more information about the International Baccalaureate.

www.qca.org.uk

This is the website of the Qualifications and Curriculum Authority. Here you can find information about the different qualifications on offer, along with details about other aspects of the 14—19 curriculum.

www.sqa.org.uk

This is the website of the Scottish Qualifications Authority. On this site you can find information about Scottish qualifications and access the parent section which provides useful information and advice.

www.accac.org.uk

This is the website of the Qualifications, Curriculum and Assessment Authority for Wales and has a useful section for parents.

www.ccea.org.uk

This is the website of the Council for the Curriculum, Examination and Assessment in Northern Ireland and has a useful section for parents.

www.lsda.org.uk

This is the website of the Learning and Skills Development Agency. It provides information on key skills and vocational learning.

Useful publications

For information about all the qualifications available in the UK, consult *British Qualifications* (2005), Kogan Page.

(3)

Understanding Study Requirements

In the previous chapter the structure of the qualification system was discussed to help overcome the confusion experienced by parents. In my research parents felt that it was also important to know more about study requirements in the different sectors, as Anne points out in the example below:

> My daughter starts university in September and I'm worried about the work she'll need to do. Will she be able to keep up? Will it be too hard for her? She's the first person to go to university from our family and I think that puts a lot of pressure on her. If I knew more about it, maybe I could help get her ready for what lies ahead.
>
> Anne, 39

Parents felt it was important to obtain more information about how their children would be taught, what work would be required of them and, in particular, what assessment procedures their children would experience.

This chapter provides information about the type of teaching methods used in colleges and universities, discussing the level and standard of work required and offering insight into the variety of assessment procedures used by educational institutions.

BECOMING FAMILIAR WITH TEACHING METHODS

The teaching methods will vary depending on the type of course, type of learning provider and preferences of tutors. The different types of teaching methods your child may encounter include the following:

♦ **Lecture** – this is formal tuition given by a lecturer to a large number of students. This often takes place in a *lecture theatre* and, in most cases, lasts for one to two hours. Students are required to listen and take notes. Questions may be invited at the end of the lecture, depending on the preferences of the tutor.

♦ **Seminar** – this is a small group discussion on a particular topic. Often students are required to present seminars themselves. To do this they will need to produce a *seminar paper* which may need to be handed in for assessment and it may count towards their final marks.

♦ **Group-work** – students may be required to work in groups on a particular project or piece of work. Sometimes this may be assessed and may count towards their final marks. Students need to work well together in the group and make sure that everyone does their fair share. Some tutors will provide guidance on effectively working together in groups.

♦ **Tutorial** – this is a small group or individual session led by a tutor to discuss a specific topic. This type of teaching method tends to be utilised more by some universities than others and is used more often during postgraduate study.

◆ **Classes** – this is a small group discussion chaired by a class tutor, usually to discuss a topic from a lecture. It provides students with the opportunity to explore the topic in more depth and ask specific questions.

◆ **Laboratory** – this is practical work associated with languages and science subjects. Students may be required to conduct their own experiments after having received careful instruction on procedures, health and safety.

◆ **Field trip** – this involves outside visits to a place or organisation that can help to clarify what is being taught. The cost of field trips may be included in the course fees, although your child should clarify this at the beginning of their course. They may be required to purchase specialised clothing and equipment for field trips, depending on the nature of their course.

◆ **Independent research** – as your child progresses with their studies, they will be required to conduct independent research. The amount of independent research required depends on the nature and level of the course. There are two types of research:

   – *Primary research* involves the study of a subject through firsthand observation and investigation, such as interviewing people or searching through statistical data. Students may be required to conduct this type of research for project work or for their *dissertation*. This is an extended piece of research carried out in the final year of a degree course.

– *Secondary research* involves the collection of information from studies that other researchers have made of a subject, such as research papers published in journals or on the internet. Students may need to conduct this type of research when carrying out group-work, conducting projects or writing essays.

STUDY REQUIREMENTS IN FURTHER EDUCATION

Further education colleges tend to provide learning opportunities for those over the compulsory school leaving age, below diploma and degree level. They provide a wide range of courses, including A Levels, NVQs and City and Guilds qualifications – some of these are academic and some are vocational courses.

All courses will require your child to undertake a certain amount of independent study, and they will be expected to complete their work on time, meeting all the deadlines set by their tutor.

The course may also involve the completion of written work, experiments, practical work, group-work, examinations and individual projects. This will mean that your child will need to develop organisation and time management skills and, if they live at home, will need to be provided with a quiet place in which to study.

The course literature should clearly explain the standard and level of work required. If you are in any doubt, speak to the course tutor or a guidance worker before your child enrols on the course. These people will be able to help you to understand whether your child will be able to meet the required standard of work.

STUDY REQUIREMENTS IN HIGHER EDUCATION

Universities offer courses at higher education level, broadly defined as any course of study leading to a qualification above Level 3 – GCE AS/A2 level and equivalents. Higher education study can be full-time or part-time and can lead to diplomas, first degrees, teaching qualifications and postgraduate degrees. Some higher education courses can lead to professional qualifications.

In theory the standard of work required should be at a higher level than your child has experienced at A Level. However, in my research with students, some have pointed out that the jump from A Level to degree level work was not as big as they had envisaged. Tutors realise that it is hard for students moving away from home and taking up university life, so they tend to break students into the new study routine gently.

As a student studying at higher education level your child will be expected to undertake a great deal of independent study without input from their tutor. They will need to complete a set number of written assignments each term or semester and they will need to successfully pass their examinations at the end of their course or module.

They will need to remain motivated throughout their course, making sure that they meet all deadlines set by tutors. They will also need to learn how to manage their time effectively and not become distracted from their studies. If they are living at home they will need to be provided with a quiet space in which to study.

Completing a dissertation

In the third year of a degree course your child may have to complete a *dissertation* which is an extended project and report (usually around 10,000 words). Your child will need to choose a relevant subject, undertake the research and analysis and complete the work by writing a report, supervised by their tutor.

BECOMING FAMILIAR WITH ASSESSMENT PROCEDURES

Assessment procedures vary, depending on the subject and level of the course. As their studies progress, your child may encounter some or all of the following types of assessment procedure.

Continual assessment

On some courses, rather than have an examination at the end, a student's progress is continually assessed. This means that, at various stages throughout the course, they have to complete an assessed piece of work. This might be a written assignment, a multiple choice questionnaire, a work-sheet, a problem, a scenario, a case study, a presentation or some other type of project.

Marking criteria may vary, but in general tutors will be looking for right answers, well-structured arguments, originality, good independent research, good grammar, punctuation and spelling.

Tutors will provide feedback on each piece of assessed work so that students can improve their technique for future work. Tutors will be able to see how your child is progressing and should be able to address any problems as they arise.

Some tutors prefer this type of assessment because they believe that examinations are not the most effective way to test a student's knowledge and understanding of a subject.

Written assignments

The length, type and number of written assignments will vary depending on the subject and level of your child's course. At college students may be expected to produce up to six assignments a year – these may be written essays, multiple choice questions, problems, scenarios or case studies to work through.

At university students may have to produce a number of written assignments for each module. These will vary in structure and length, depending on the course.

Students will be provided with a timetable of assignment deadlines at the beginning of the course and must adhere to these deadlines. In exceptional circumstances they may be able to apply for extensions, but will need to show that they have a very good reason for the extension to be granted.

Marking criteria vary, but in general tutors will be looking for a well-researched, original and imaginative piece of work, free from spelling and grammatical errors. It should be well-structured with a clear introduction and conclusion. References should be clearly marked and included in the bibliography.

Plagiarism is the unauthorised use or copying of other people's work without acknowledgement. Many universities now use electronic plagiarism detectors and if a student is caught out they could be failed or asked to leave their course. All tutors should provide clear advice on avoiding plagiarism.

Group project work

Some colleges and universities mark their students on their group project work, awarding the same mark for all members of that group for their work. This means that the group must work well together and produce a good piece of work if they are going to receive a high mark. Some tutors will provide guidelines on working together in groups and they will offer advice to a group that is not working efficiently.

If your child has a problem with a particular group, or member of a group, they should raise any concerns as soon as possible so that the assessed group project does not have a detrimental effect on their overall mark.

Presentations

On some courses students will be required to make a presentation on a chosen piece of work. The presentation may be assessed and count towards their final mark. At college students may be required to make a presentation to fellow classmates and the tutor. At university students may be required to present a seminar – the tutor may assess both the standard of presentation and the written seminar paper.

Marking criteria vary, but tutors will be looking for a well-researched presentation, which is logically and clearly organised. Tutors understand that students may be nervous and will not mark them down for nerves. However, they may be looking for good, competent use of visual aids.

Examinations

As your child is thinking about college or university they should, by now, be used to examinations. However, procedures may differ when they are at college or university so they should become familiar with these before they take any exams.

Some courses no longer have examinations as an assessment procedure because tutors feel that they are not the most effective way to test students' learning.

Examination arrangements for students with disabilities

College and universities may allow extra examination time on medical grounds, such as dyslexia, injury or disability. If your child has any medical condition that may influence their ability to take examinations, they will need to make sure that they obtain a letter from their course director and take it with them to the exam. They will need to show the invigilator that they are entitled to extra time and should make sure that they use any extra time to which they are entitled.

Alternative examination arrangements may be available for students with other disabilities. These depend upon your child's requirements and may include the arrangements listed below.

- Additional time and extra reading time.
- Rest breaks.
- Flexible starting time.
- Personal assistance, such as a scribe, reader or interpreter.
- Specialist equipment, such as computers, dictionaries and furniture.
- Large print, Braille or audio-tape exam papers.
- A separate venue.

KNOWING ABOUT ACADEMIC APPEAL PROCEDURES

If, during their studies, your child is unhappy with the course or the way they have been assessed, they are able to consider making an appeal.

However, your child first needs to decide whether they wish to make an *appeal* or a *complaint*. An appeal is a request for a review of a decision made by the examination board charged with making decisions on student progression and assessments. A complaint is a specific concern about the provision of a programme of study or related academic services.

Making an appeal

All colleges and universities have procedures in place for students who wish to appeal against the results they have been given for assessed pieces of work and for examinations. However, your child will not be able to appeal just because you or they believe they should have been awarded a higher mark.

Although rules and regulations vary, in general your child will be allowed to appeal in the following circumstances:

◆ There was an administrative error, breach of regulations or procedural irregularity during the conduct of the assessment.

◆ Circumstances existed which, for exceptional reasons, could not be communicated to the examination board before it reached its decision. This may include illness or a personal crisis. All circumstances will need to be supported by written evidence.

Colleges and universities will provide information about their specific appeal procedure in the student handbook. Some students' unions appoint an officer or full-time member of staff to help students through the appeal procedure.

Making a complaint

If your child is unhappy with part of the course or academic services, they should first of all discuss their concerns informally with their tutor or supervisor. If they are still unhappy they can approach their student representative or visit their students' union. These people will be able to offer advice about the specific complaints procedures as these vary between colleges and universities.

If your child is unable to resolve the matter informally, most colleges and universities appoint a *complaints officer* who will be able to deal directly with your child's formal complaint. This person will investigate the complaint and provide a written report on their conclusions. More information will be available in your child's student handbook.

USEFUL INFORMATION

Useful websites

www.bbc.co.uk/education/asguru
This website provides useful advice and information on revising for AS Levels.

www.open.ac.uk/study-strategies
This is the Open University website and provides useful study tips in the areas of language skills, taking examinations, planning studies, and reading and reviewing information.

Useful publications

If your child is interested in improving their study skills before they go away to college or university, they may find the following publications useful:

Burt, A. (2004) *Quick Solutions to Common Errors in English*, 3rd edition. How To Books.

Burt, A. (2003) *Write with Confidence*. How To Books.

Dawson, C. (2005) *A Practical Guide to Research Methods – a user friendly manual for mastering research techniques and projects*, 2nd edition. How To Books.

Dawson, C. (2004) *Learning How to Study Again*. How To Books.

Field, M. (2003) *Improve Your Punctuation and Grammar*, 2nd edition. How To Books.

Field, M. (2000) *Improve Your Spelling*. How To Books.

Smith, P. (2002) *Writing an Assignment*, 5th edition. How To Books.

Swetnam, D. (2003) *Writing Your Dissertation*, 3rd edition. How To Books.

4

Obtaining Government Financial Support

The system of government financial support for students has changed considerably over the last few years. Many parents feel that this system is confusing and it is hard for them to understand what funds, if any, are available for their children, as Ellen points out:

> Higher education is suffering because it is such a worry and struggle to go to university that just the thought puts people off...why can't she claim income support to help? She will be living away from home solely responsible for herself. I don't believe I will still be able to claim for her; instead she will have to go into debt. What a way to start your journey through working life. Does the state still have some support for these students trying to better themselves?
>
> Ellen (single parent)

In my research parents reported that lack of money and fears of student debt are creating the greatest concern about their child continuing their studies.

This chapter explains the government system of financial support for further and higher education, discussing learner support funds, tuition fees, student loans, the parental contribution and benefits. Information about applying for these funds is provided along with details about how to obtain the relevant application forms.

OBTAINING FUNDING FOR FURTHER EDUCATION COURSES

There are several types of funding available if your child wishes to continue into further education after they have finished their compulsory schooling. However, you should note that these schemes may not be offered in all parts of the UK and the administration and eligibility criteria can vary.

To obtain more specific information you should contact your LEA (England and Wales). If you live in Northern Ireland or Scotland relevant contact details appear at the end of this chapter.

Tuition fees/course fees (UK)

Most students between the ages of 16–19 studying at school sixth forms or further education colleges will not have to pay tuition fees or course fees. Also, at some colleges they may not be required to pay enrolment and examination fees. Only students attending private schools or colleges will have to pay course fees.

The School Learner Support Fund (England and Wales)

This fund provides small grants to students in school sixth forms if their ability to start or complete the course is inhibited by financial constraints. The fund is adminis-tered by LEAs and may be given as a grant each term, as a one-off sum to cover exceptional course costs, or as an individual hardship grant administered at the beginning of term.

Funds are available only to students between the ages of 16 and 19. There is no automatic entitlement to funding – each applicant is judged individually and funds are not guaranteed.

The College Learner Support Fund (England and Wales)

This fund is available for students studying at further education colleges who are in severe financial need. The funds are administered by colleges and are given usually as one-off grants when students are experiencing severe financial hardship.

Your child can apply for these funds at any time of the year once they have started their course. They should contact the *student support officer* at their college for more information and an application form.

Specialist Residential Colleges (England)

This scheme is available for students who choose to study at one of 51 designated specialist colleges. A list of the designated colleges can be obtained from the booklet *Financial Help for Students.* You can obtain a copy of this booklet by telephoning 0845 6022260.

If your child wishes to study at one of these colleges, they should contact the college and ask for details of the bursary scheme. Financial help is available for two or three years depending on the length of the course.

Residential Pilot Scheme (England)

This scheme is available if your child is aged 16 or over and they are studying, or about to study, full-time at Level

3. Funds are available for study on a specialist course that is not available within daily travel distance of your home.

To qualify for this scheme your child must be 'ordinarily resident' in England. Colleges and courses taking part in this scheme can be found at www.aimhigher.ac.uk. Applications are made through the college.

Local Education Awards (England and Wales)

Some LEAs offer grants and bursaries to local residents attending specified courses at eligible institutions. These are usually lump sums paid at the beginning of the course. They are income-assessed and offered to students who may be unable to take up their studies because of financial constraints.

To be eligible your child will need to pass certain residence conditions and provide proof of their family financial circumstances. In some areas your child will automatically qualify for payment if you are in receipt of Income Support.

Teachers at your child's school can request information and application forms for all schemes administered by your LEA, so check first whether this information is available from their school. Alternatively, you can contact the *Student Support* section of your LEA for more information and application forms. Most LEAs accept applications from the April before the start of the academic year.

Assembly Learning Grant (Wales)

Welsh students can apply for this grant if they are from a low income family. Your child must be following a post-compulsory education course of least 275 hours a year which leads to a nationally recognised qualification. Your permanent home must be in Wales but your child may be entitled to receive the grant if they study elsewhere in the UK. Applications are made through your LEA.

Passport to Study Grant (Wales)

In Wales some LEAs award these grants to 16-19 year olds who stay on in full-time education. The money is for expenses such as books, travel and equipment. Contact your LEA or visit www.elwa.ac.uk for more information.

FE bursary (Scotland)

All full-time students in FE colleges in Scotland can apply for a non-repayable bursary to help with living costs. The amount of bursary your child will receive depends upon your family income and they have to meet certain rules to be eligible. Awards are discretionary and your child should speak to their college *bursary officer* to find out whether they are eligible.

FE awards (Northern Ireland)

In Northern Ireland students studying on programmes of study that are not eligible for mandatory funding can apply for discretionary awards. However, funds are limited so the Education and Library Boards (ELBs) try to ensure that the funds are distributed in a fair and equitable manner. Your child should contact their ELB or learning provider for more information.

The Education Maintenance Allowance (EMA)

This scheme became fully functional in September 2004. It is available in England, Wales and Northern Ireland. In Scotland the scheme is being introduced on a stepped basis to be fully functional by 2007/08.

Through this income-assessed scheme students from low income families who decide to continue their education are offered up to £30 a week plus periodic bonuses. EMAs are available for A Level courses and vocational courses.

Your child can request details and application forms from your LEA or school. Alternatively, application forms and guidance information can be requested or downloaded from the DfES website listed at the end of this chapter.

Transport costs (UK)

Help with transport costs is available for students aged 16–19. To find out what help is available in your area contact your LEA (England and Wales), ELB (Northern Ireland) or SAAS (Scotland).

Students with disabilities and special needs (UK)

There are a variety of schemes available if your child has a disability and/or special needs. Some bus companies offer free travel and some LEAs arrange free transport. Many LEAs employ a person who deals with funding applications for disabled students and these people will be able to provide you with details of local schemes (see Chapter 8).

OBTAINING FUNDING FOR HIGHER EDUCATION COURSES

If your child depends on you financially there are several types of government financial support available to them.

Financial support schemes vary in different parts of the UK so if you are in doubt you should seek further information from the relevant authorities.

Tuition fees (England, Wales and Northern Ireland)
Since 1998 full-time students studying on higher education courses have had to make a contribution towards their tuition fees. The remainder of the cost of their course is automatically paid by the government. However, if you are on a low income your child will not have to pay any tuition fees. In the academic year 2005/06 their contribution towards tuition fees will be £1,175.

Once your child has been offered a place at university they will be given a date by which time their fees have to be paid. This is usually at the start of the course. Some universities will accept payment in instalments.

Applications for help with tuition fees are made through your LEA (England and Wales) or ELB (Northern Ireland).

Changes to tuition fees in England
In 2006/07 universities in England will be able to decide how much they are going to charge, up to £3,000, and these fee levels should be displayed clearly in prospectuses and on websites. However, these new variable rates only apply to new students. If your child is a second or third year student in 2006, their tuition fees will be £1,200.

From 2006 your child will be able to pay their tuition fees after they have finished their studies. During their course they can take out a fee loan from the Student Loans

Company to cover fees. This will be paid back after graduation with the rest of the student loan. The loans will still be repaid at the same rate (nine per cent of their salary above £15,000), but it will take them longer to repay the loan.

At the time of writing, MPs have voted for a similar system of top-up fees in Northern Ireland, although it is yet to be made law.

Tuition fees (Scotland)
If you live in Scotland and your child intends to study at a Scottish institution, the Student Awards Agency for Scotland (SAAS) will pay their tuition fees. If your child intends to study elsewhere in the UK, the SAAS will assess their entitlement to help with tuition fees. This will depend upon your family income.

If your child is eligible for help with their tuition fees, the SAAS will pay their fees direct to the college or university. Applications are made through the SAAS.

Young Students' Bursaries (Scotland)
These are available for Scottish students under the age of 25 from low income families. The amount of bursary your child will receive depends upon your family income. The bursary is paid in three instalments direct into your child's bank account. Applications are made through the SAAS.

Student loans (UK)
Anyone under 50, on a full-time, higher education course can apply for a student loan if they meet the residence requirements. This means that your child must have been

living in the UK, the Channel Islands or the Isle of Man for the three years immediately before the start of the academic year in which their course begins. Students applying for sandwich and part-time initial teacher training courses are also eligible to apply.

Your child will not have to start repaying their loan until the April after they have left or finished their course, and the amount they repay will be linked to their income. They will not have to make repayments while their income is below the threshold of £15,000. Interest on their loan is linked to inflation, so the amount they repay will be worth what they borrowed.

Applications for student loans are made through your LEA or online (England and Wales), ELB (Northern Ireland) and SAAS (Scotland).

Once your child's university has confirmed to the SLC that they are attending the relevant course, they will receive their first loan instalment. For most students this will be direct into their bank or building society account.

Higher Education Grant (England and Wales)
A means-tested grant of up to £1,000 for students from low income families was introduced in September 2004. The grant is paid by the Student Loans Company in three instalments over the academic year. This grant will be replaced by the Maintenance Grant in 2006.

Maintenance Grant (England and Wales)
As part of the new arrangements to be introduced in 2006, the government is offering a Maintenance Grant of up to

£2,700 for students from low income families. This will replace the Higher Education Grant offered in 2005. For Welsh students, this grant will include the Assembly Learning Grant.

Your child will be able to apply for this grant when they apply for their student support from your LEA or online.

Assembly Learning Grant (Wales)
If you live in Wales your child may be eligible to apply for this grant if you are on a low income. Your permanent home must be in Wales but your child may be entitled to receive the grant if they study elsewhere in the UK. Applications are made through your LEA.

Higher Education Bursaries (Northern Ireland)
These are available for students from low income families in Northern Ireland. The amount of bursary your child will receive depends upon your family income. The bursary is paid in three instalments direct into your child's bank account. Applications are made through your ELB.

Hardship funds (UK)
These are special funds offered by colleges and universities to students who are facing financial hardship. In England they are called *Access to Learning Funds*, in Scotland they are called *Hardship Funds,* in Northern Ireland they are called *Support Funds* and in Wales they are called *Financial Contingency Funds*.

These funds are available for both full-time and part-time students to help with course-related costs such as books, equipment, childcare and general living costs. Each applicant is assessed individually – your child may be required to show evidence of your family income when they make an application. Payment will usually be made as one-off grants. There is no automatic entitlement to money from these funds.

Once your child has taken up their place with their chosen learning provider, they should contact the *student service* or *welfare department* as soon as possible to find out about available funds. They will only be eligible for these funds if they can prove that they have applied for the full student loan. Their Students' Union or university welfare officer will be able to offer further advice.

PAYING THE PARENTAL CONTRIBUTION

If your child is financially dependent on you and your income is over a certain amount, the government expects you to help make a contribution towards their tuition fees and living costs while they are studying at university.

To work out the level of parental contribution, your residual income is taken into account. This is done by taking your gross income (before tax and national insurance) and taking off various allowances.

The residual income will be worked out for the previous financial year. However, if your income has fallen significantly over the last financial year you can ask that the current year is taken into account instead.

If you are separated, the income of the parent with whom your child lives will be assessed. If you have remarried, entered into a civil partnership, or live with a partner (of the same or opposite sex), their income will also be taken into account when the parental contribution is worked out.

KNOWING ABOUT BENEFITS

Most full-time students are not entitled to claim social security benefits. However, students from certain vulnerable groups such as those listed below may be able to claim some benefits:

- lone parents
- disabled people
- students intercalating after a period of sickness or caring.

Full-time students are only eligible to apply for Housing Benefit if they meet one of the following conditions:

- They are in receipt of Income Support or income-based Job Seekers' Allowance. (Most full-time students cannot claim these benefits, although it may be possible if your child has been unemployed for some time and is studying as part of the New Deal programme).

- They are a lone parent with a child under 16.

- They are classed as a 'disabled student'.

- They have temporarily suspended their studies due to ill health or caring responsibilities.

Since September 2004, if your child is from one of the vulnerable groups described above and lives in university-owned accommodation, they may be eligible to apply for Housing Benefit during the term-time.

Benefits for part-time students

If your child is intending to study on a part-time course and is claiming benefits, they should check with their Jobcentre Plus office, as their benefits may be affected by their studies. However, they may be entitled to some benefits as the part-time grant is not considered to be enough to affect benefits.

Benefit rules can be complicated and you are advised to seek specialist advice relevant to your child's specific circumstances. More information can be obtained from your Jobcentre Plus office, Benefits Office, Benefit helpline (0800 88 22 00) or from www.dwp.gov.uk/lifeevent/benefits.

Benefits claimed by parents

As a parents or carer you will continue to receive child benefit and other benefits already claimed if your child remains in full-time education up to the age of 19.

USEFUL INFORMATION

Useful addresses

The head office of the Learning and Skills Council is:

Learning and Skills Council (Head Office)

101 Lockhurst Lane

Foleshill

Coventry CV6 5RS

General enquiries: 0870 9006 800

Fax: 02476 703 314

Email: info@lsc.gov.uk

If you want to find out more about student loans, contact:
Student Loans Company Limited
100 Bothwell Street
Glasgow G2 7JD
Tel: 0800 405 010
Website: www.slc.co.uk

If you live in Scotland, more information about student financial support and application forms can be obtained from the Student Awards Agency for Scotland:
The Student Awards Agency for Scotland
3 Redheughs Rigg
South Gyle
Edinburgh EH12 9YT
Tel: 0131 476 8212
Website: www.saas.gov.uk.

If you live in Northern Ireland you can obtain more information and an application form from your local Education and Library Board. Alternatively, you can contact the Department for Employment and Learning:
Department for Employment and Learning
Student Finance Branch
Room 407
Adelaide House
39–49 Adelaide Street
Belfast BT2 8FD
Tel: 028 9025 7728
Website: www.delni.gov.uk

If you live in England or Wales, contact your LEA for more information and an application form. Alternatively, you can obtain more information from the Department for Education and Science:

Department for Education and Science
Sanctuary Buildings
Great Smith Street
London SW1P 3BT
Tel: 0870 000 2288
Website: www.dfes.gov.uk

Useful websites

www.dfes.gov.uk/studentsupport
This website provides information about all aspects of student finance in England and Wales.

www.studentfinancedirect.co.uk
Students in England and Wales can apply online for financial support through this website.

www.dfes.gov.uk/financialhelp/ema
This website provides information about the Education Maintenance Allowance in England and Wales.

www.emascotland.com
This website contains information about the Education Maintenance Allowance in Scotland.

www.learning.wales.gov.uk
www.elwa.ac.uk
For Welsh students in 2006/07, responsibility for student support will be transferred from the DfES to the National Assembly for Wales. More information can be obtained from these websites.

www.entitledto.co.uk

This website provides a free web-based calculator to help people work out their entitlement to benefits and tax credits.

Useful publications

For students in further education the Department for Education and Skills has produced two booklets called *Money to Learn* and *Financial Help for Students*. You can obtain copies by contacting:

DfES Publications

PO Box 5050

Sherwood Park

Annesley

Nottingham NG15 0DJ

Tel: 0845 60 222 60

Email: dfes@prolog.uk.com

Further information about the system of government financial support for higher education can be obtained from the guide *Financial Support for Higher Education Students*. The guide can be obtained from the DfES website above, by telephoning 0800 731 9133 or by contacting your Local Education Authority (England and Wales). Students in Northern Ireland should contact their ELB for this publication.

A booklet called *Student Loans: A Guide to Terms and Conditions* can be obtained from the Student Loans Company information line: 0800 731 9133.

(5)

Finding Other Sources of Income

In addition to the government financial support discussed in the previous chapter, there are other sources of funding available if your child wishes to continue their studies at college or university. However, it can be difficult to find out about this type of funding, as Penny points out:

> I had heard that there was some money available from a charity in our area. But when I tried to find out about it, it was like I was hitting my head against a brick wall. I just didn't know where to start and nobody seemed able to help me.
>
> Penny, 41

Some of the extra funding available is for specific types of courses, such as courses in healthcare or social work. Other funding is available through educational trusts and charities or through university scholarships and company sponsorship.

This chapter provides details of this additional funding, along with advice about how to obtain more information and apply for funding. All figures relate to the academic year 2005/06 unless otherwise stated.

FUNDING FOR HEALTHCARE STUDENTS

If your child is interested in studying on a healthcare

course, a bursary is available from the National Health Service (NHS). There are two types of bursary available and the one your child will receive depends upon the course they intend to study:

◆ **Means Tested Bursary** – this is available for degree level courses and postgraduate level courses in healthcare. The amount of bursary your child will receive depends upon your income.

◆ **Non-means Tested Bursary** – if your child intends to study on a nursing, midwifery or operating department practitioner diploma course, they will be entitled to apply for a full bursary. The amount they will receive does not depend upon your income.

In addition to these bursaries there are various other allowances for which your child will be able to apply, depending upon their personal circumstances. These include allowances for:

◆ extra week's Attendance
◆ older students
◆ dependants
◆ single parents
◆ disabled students
◆ second homes
◆ practice placement costs.

Medicine and dentistry

If your child plans to study medicine or dentistry in any UK country, they should apply for the financial support discussed in Chapter 4 for the first four years of study. For subsequent years of study, funding is available from the NHS.

Applying for an NHS Bursary

When your child has been offered an NHS funded place, their college will advise the relevant authority of the offer. Your child will be sent a bursary application pack. They should complete and return the form, attaching all requested documentation.

When your child begins their training, they will be sent a letter advising them of the level of bursary they are due to receive.

FUNDING FOR TEACHER TRAINING

If your child wishes to train to become a teacher by studying for a Bachelor of Education degree (BEd), they are eligible to apply for the type of government financial support described in Chapter 4. However, to help encourage people into teaching, there are extra incentives available:

* **Tuition fees (Scotland)** – if your child is a Scottish student wishing to study on a teacher training course in Scotland, they will have their tuition fees paid for them.

* **Secondary Shortage Subject Scheme (England)** – the details of this scheme change each year so your child will need to check the availability for the year in which they are interested. Through this scheme students may be provided with an income-assessed grant of up to £5,000 for those under 25 years of age. Applications are made through your child's teacher-training provider.

- **Secondary Undergraduate Placement Grant (Wales)** – a grant of £1,000 is offered to undergraduate students studying in Wales in one of the secondary priority subjects. For those studying other subjects, £600 is available. The funds are to help with the cost of school placements. Applications are made through your child's teacher-training provider.

Postgraduate teacher training

If your child intends to study to become a teacher through the postgraduate route, that is studying first for a degree and then for a postgraduate teacher training qualification, there are several sources of funding available:

- **Tuition fees (UK)** – your child can get all their tuition fees paid and will not need to repay this money. Applications are made through your LEA (England and Wales), ELB (Northern Ireland) or SAAS (Scotland). Relevant addresses are provided in Chapter 4.

- **Teacher Bursary (England)** – a bursary of £6,000 for the year is offered to graduates who enrol on a course leading to qualified teacher status; £7,000 is offered to maths and science trainees. Applications are made through the teacher training college.

- **Secondary Shortage Subject Scheme (England)** – this is similar to the scheme for undergraduates (see above).

- **Teacher training incentives (Wales)** – if your child intends to study on a postgraduate course that leads to qualified teacher status in Wales, they may be eligible for a £6,000 training grant or a £7,000 training grant for maths and science trainees. Applications for the training grant are made through your child's teacher training college.

◆ **Teaching Grants (Wales)** – upon successful completion of their teacher training course in Wales, your child may be entitled to an extra teaching grant of £5,000 (maths and science) or £4,000 for other priority subject areas. Applications are made through the Welsh Assembly.

◆ **PGCE (FE) Bursary Pilot Scheme (Wales)** – a grant of £6,000 is offered to students at designated Welsh higher education institutions who intend to teach in further education. Applications and payments are arranged by the college or university.

FUNDING FOR DANCE AND DRAMA

Dance and Drama Awards are available for talented students who wish to become professional dancers, actors or stage managers. The Awards offer greatly reduced tuition fees and help with living and learning costs. The level of funding depends upon your family income.

Dance and Drama Awards are offered at further education level. If your child's course is at higher education level they will need to apply for the type of funding described in Chapter 4.

Funding is available for students in England, Wales and Scotland. If you live in Northern Ireland you should contact your local ELB for more information.

Applying for Dance and Drama Awards

Your child should contact the dance and drama training

provider in which they are interested, requesting a prospectus, an application form and information about the Awards.

Once they have applied to the college they will be invited to attend an audition and interview. They should inform the college at this time that they wish to apply for an Award.

The Awards will be allocated according to talent displayed at the audition. However, if applicants are thought to be of equal talent, funds will be allocated according to individual financial circumstances.

FUNDING FOR FINE AND PERFORMING ARTS

The *Leverhulme Trust* offers a limited number of scholarships and bursaries for students in the fine and performing arts. These are available for talented students who wish to continue their professional development and training in these areas.

Funds are normally offered for a maximum of three years and the amount your child will receive depends on personal circumstances and need. Applications must be made through the institution to which they have applied.

If your child is interested in this funding they should contact their chosen institution to find out whether there are any funds available.

FUNDING FOR SOCIAL WORK

Financial support is available to both undergraduate and postgraduate students who are studying on an approved course in social work.

Most social work undergraduate students receive the same help as other undergraduate students (see Chapter 4). However, there are extra schemes available to help encourage people to train for, and work within, shortage areas. These schemes vary throughout the UK. For more information and application forms you should contact the relevant organisation:

Welsh students should contact the Care Council for Wales:
6th Floor
South Gate House
Wood Street
Cardiff CF10 1EW
Tel: 029 2022 6257
Email: info@ccwales.org.uk
Website: www.ccwales.org.uk

Scottish students should contact the Scottish Social Services Council:
Compass House
11 Riverside Drive
Dundee DD1 4NY
Tel: 0845 60 30 891
Email: enquiries@sssc.uk.com
Website: www.sssc.uk.com

Students in Northern Ireland should contact the Social Services Inspectorate:
C4
Castle Buildings
Stormont
Tel: 028 9052 0517

Email: dorothy.vance@dhsspsni.gov.uk
Website: www.dhsspsni.gov.uk

English students should contact the General Social Care Council:
Bursaries Office, General Social Care Council
Goldings House
2 Hay's Lane
London SE1 2HB
Tel: 020 7397 5835
Email: bursaries@gscc.org.uk
Website: www.gscc.org.uk

UNIVERSITY STUDENTSHIPS AND BURSARIES

Most universities offer sums of money to certain students studying at their institution. The amount and type of award varies between institutions, as do the conditions and application procedures. Also, institutions might use a variety of names for the different types of funding, such as 'scholarships', 'studentships', 'grants' or 'bursaries'.

From 2006 universities must have an access agreement with the Office for Fair Access (OFFA). This has been established to try to ensure that underrepresented groups can access higher education, despite the increases in tuition fees. Universities will provide a limited number of bursaries for students on low incomes if they intend to charge more than £2,700 in fees.

All universities will have to clearly advertise the number and level of bursaries available in their prospectuses and on their websites. If you are on a low income, make contact with your child's chosen university and find out what bursaries are available. Application packs and guidelines can be obtained direct from the university.

FUNDING FOR SPORTS

Funding may be available if your child excels at a particular sport and wishes to study at university whilst participating in their sport. Scholarships and bursaries are available for students who display exceptional talent for their chosen sport.

Eligibility criteria, application procedures and amount of funding vary according to the type of bursary or scholarship. However, most bursaries will be offered on the basis of financial need, performance, actual skill or expected potential. Contact colleges and universities for more information.

OBTAINING COMPANY SPONSORSHIP

Some companies are willing to sponsor students through their studies by providing an agreed sum of money for one, two, three or four years of study. Contracts will vary considerably. If a company offers a significant amount of money, employers will expect your child to work for them for a certain number of years after completing their studies.

However, this type of sponsorship is now quite rare. Instead, companies tend to offer smaller sums, providing working opportunities through vacations and during sandwich years. This type of sponsorship tends not to tie your child into working for the company once they have graduated, although many students find that they are offered a job upon successful completion of their course.

If your child is sponsored by the Armed Services, they will generally be expected to serve for a set period of time after graduation. Also, they may be expected to attend weekend training sessions and summer camps. If they leave any one of the Armed Services before the service commitment is concluded, they can be asked to repay the whole of the cash advance.

Applying for company sponsorship

Applications will need to be made directly to the company or Armed Service in which your child is interested. Many companies will want to know that your child has been offered a university place before they will consider sponsoring them.

However, some companies work closely with specific universities – if your child knows they want to follow this route, they should contact the company in which they are interested prior to making their UCAS application.

FUNDING FROM EDUCATIONAL TRUSTS AND CHARITIES

Throughout the UK there are a number of local and national educational trusts and charities that offer bursaries and grants for study at further and higher education institutions. The funds have been set aside by individuals or corporations to help specific kinds of people and may be available to help with costs such as maintenance, fees, books, equipment, travel and field trips.

Sometimes local trusts and charities can be a useful source of income if you have lived in an area for a long time. Visit your local library, local clergy or Citizens' Advice Bureau for more information.

Finding information about trusts and charities

The Educational Grants Advisory Service is an independent advice agency for people who want to obtain funding for further or higher education. It is concerned mainly with providing advice for people who are not eligible for government funding, although it will provide advice on grants and loans if requested.

Educational Grants Advisory Service (EGAS)
501–505 Kingsland Road
Dalston
London E8 4AU
Information line: 020 7254 6251

Applying to trusts and charities

If your child decides to apply to an educational trust or charity they should first of all make sure that they have exhausted all sources of statutory funding. Trusts and charities will want to know that they have done this and will ask for details of any refusals.

Most trusts and charities will provide an application form. When your child fills in this form, they should tailor their application to suit the charity and make sure that they provide all the detail requested. They should be honest and realistic and not be too emotional.

Your child should be encouraged to write neatly, be concise and avoid jargon. If they fail in one application, they should try another to increase their chances of being successful. However, you must note that funds are limited and it can be difficult to obtain financial support from these sources.

USEFUL INFORMATION

Useful addresses

For enquiries concerning NHS financial support in England you should contact:

NHS Student Grants Unit

22 Plymouth Road

Blackpool FY3 7JS

Tel: 01253 655 655

Website: www.nhspa.gov.uk

For enquiries concerning NHS financial support in Wales you should contact:

NHS Wales Student Awards Unit

2nd Floor

Golate House

101 St. Mary's Street

Cardiff CF10 1DX

Tel: 029 2026 1495

For enquiries concerning NHS financial support in Scotland you should contact:

The Student Awards Agency for Scotland

3 Redheughs Rigg

South Gyle

Edinburgh EH12 9YT

Tel: 0845 111 1711

Website: www.saas.gov.uk

For enquiries concerning NHS financial support in Northern Ireland you should contact:

North Eastern Education and Library Board

County Hall

182 Galgorm Road
Ballymena
County Antrim BT42 1HN
Tel: 028 2565 3333
Website: www.neelb.org.uk

Advice about careers and funding in dance and drama can be obtained from the following organisations. On their websites you can find details of the courses that attract funding, along with information about how and when to apply, including useful tips on coping with an audition.

Council for Dance Education and Training (CDET)
Toynbee Hall
28 Commercial Street
London E1 6LS
Answers for Dancers information line 0901 800 0014
E-mail: info@cdet.org.uk
Website: www.cdet.org.uk

National Council for Drama Training
1–7 Woburn Walk
London WC1H 0JJ
Tel: 020 7387 3650
E-mail: info@ncdt.co.uk
Website: www.ncdt.co.uk

Useful websites

www.dfes.gov.uk/financialhelp/dancedrama
More information about Dance and Drama Awards can be obtained from this website.

www.scholarship-search.org.uk

Information about university awards can be obtained from Scholarship Search UK. This site provides a free search facility for all students who want to study at university in the UK. The undergraduate database covers scholarships, sponsorships, prizes and hardship awards and aims to be as comprehensive as possible.

www.iefa.org

This is the International Education Financial Aid website. If your child is interested in obtaining sports scholarships abroad they can consult this site for details.

www.funderfinder.org.uk

Once your child starts college or university, they can visit the *student support offices*. Most will provide access to computer databases such as *Funderfinder* which is a software package that provides a quick and easy way of finding out which charitable trusts might be able to help. Details of this database can be found on the website above.

www.nusonline.co.uk

This is the website of the National Union of Students. Further information about educational trusts and charities can be obtained from this site.

www.rafcareers.com

Visit this site for more information about careers in the RAF and sponsorship deals.

www.royal-marines.mod.uk
www.royal-navy.mod.uk

These websites provide more information about a career and sponsorship opportunities in the Royal Navy or the Royal Marines.

www.armyofficer.co.uk

www.armygrants.co.uk

Visit these sites for more information about joining the Army as an officer and for sponsorship opportunities.

Useful publications

The Department of Health booklet *Financial Help for Healthcare Students* explains NHS funding in more detail and can be obtained from:

Department of Health

PO Box 777

London SE1 6XH

Tel: 08701 555 455

Website: www.doh.gov.uk

The Sponsorship and Funding Directory (published by Hobsons) lists scholarships and bursaries available for students. The book should be available in your local library. It contains a comprehensive list of funding bodies and provides corporate profiles, outlining sponsorship opportunities available with these companies.

You may also find the following books useful:

CRAC (2004) *Student Support Sponsorship Funding Directory 2005*. Hobsons.

Harland, S. and Griffiths, D. (2004) *The Educational Grants Directory 2004/5*. Directory of Social Change.

6

Planning Your Expenditure

During my research parents pointed out that they were concerned about how much it was going to cost for their children to go away to college or university. Of greatest concern were course and tuition fees, accommodation, course materials and books, as the following quotation from Alison illustrates:

> I really am worried about how much it will all cost. I don't earn a lot and my ex-husband won't pay. How much will her accommodation be? What about the fees? I know books are expensive and what about all the other stuff she will have to buy? How on earth do I work out how much all that will cost?
>
> Alison, 48

In addition to these costs there are other items you will have to consider when you are helping your child to plan their expenditure. These include insurance, council tax, IT equipment, photocopying, laser printing and travel.

In this chapter each of these issues is discussed so that, as parents, you can obtain a greater understanding of the type of expenditure you and your child may need to face when your child goes away to college or university.

PAYING COURSE/TUITION FEES

Most students between the ages of 16–19 studying at

school sixth forms or further education colleges will not have to pay course fees.

Only students attending private schools or private colleges will have to pay course fees. These fees vary enormously and you should consult individual prospectuses for more information.

University tuition fees

If your child is going to university they will have to pay tuition fees (see Chapter 4). In the academic year 2005/06 their contribution towards tuition fees will be £1,175.

In 2006/07 universities will be able to decide how much they are going to charge, up to £3,000, and these fee levels should be displayed clearly in prospectuses and on websites. Some universities intend to charge the full amount, whereas others may charge less than £3,000.

These new variable rates only apply to new students. If your child is a second or third year student in 2006, their tuition fees will be £1,200 for that year.

Up until 2006 tuition fees have to be paid at the start of your child's course, although some universities may let your child pay fees in instalments. From 2006 your child will be able to pay their tuition fees after they have finished their studies. To do this they will be able to take out an additional student loan to cover their tuition fees.

PAYING FOR ACCOMMODATION

Accommodation costs depend upon the type of accommodation your child chooses and the place in which they intend to study. The two main types of accommodation chosen by students are in university-owned halls of residence or in private rented accommodation.

Halls of residence

The price of university accommodation depends upon the type of rooms available and whether your child chooses catered or self-catered halls. Most universities now have a selection of accommodation to suit all tastes and budgets, and many institutions give first choice and priority to first year students.

Perhaps surprisingly, accommodation costs do not vary a great deal between geographical locations. Instead, they vary between *types* of accommodation and the facilities available. For example, for a basic, non-catered room without internet access you could expect to pay £40–£55 a week. For a top of the range, en-suite room with internet connection you could expect to pay £65–£80 a week.

In most cases the more expensive accommodation tends to be en-suite with internet access available in each room. The more you pay the more facilities your child tends to receive – some halls have their own launderettes, television rooms, computing rooms and so on.

If you are on a budget you need to think about how many of these facilities your child actually needs. Sometimes the cheaper halls might be better – they may not have many facilities, but they may have a better communal spirit because students understand the need to budget, are able to support each other and are happy to arrange cheap entertainment and social activities for themselves.

Paying for halls of residence

In general, rent covers heating, lighting, water and cleaning. However, some students are now expected to clean their own rooms which are then inspected at the end of term. If your child has chosen a catered hall, meals may be included in the overall price.

Most universities enable student to pay their rent in three ways:

◆ Single payment by invoice for full period. Payment can be made by cash, cheque, credit/debit card.

◆ Payment each term as invoiced. Payment can be made by cash, cheque, credit/debit card.

◆ Payment by direct debit.

When your child chooses a place to study they should be encouraged to think carefully about the type of accommodation they can afford and the sort of accommodation in which they would be happy. This is because most universities will charge students for changing if they are unhappy. You can arrange to visit halls prior to your child making their choice.

Private rented accommodation

Private accommodation rents vary considerably over the country and within specific areas of towns and cities. If your child chooses to live in a fashionable part of the city, rent could be twice as much as it would be in a less fashionable area.

Most towns and cities have areas within them that are popular with students. In general, these tend to be areas of terraced houses that can provide rooms for four or five students in each property, located within walking distance of the college or university. Your child can expect to pay the following weekly rent for this type of property:

◆ London £65–£75
◆ Leeds £40–£55
◆ Newcastle £35–£50
◆ Southampton £50–£60

Obviously, the more your child shops around the better deal they are likely to get. In some popular student areas properties might be advertised from as early as January for the autumn term, so your child has to begin looking early.

Deposits
All landlords will ask for a deposit to protect them against any damage that might occur to their property. This usually ranges from £200–£300 or is equivalent to the rent for one month.

Letting agency fees
Letting agencies are not allowed to charge a registration fee for finding accommodation. However, they can make a charge once a client has accepted accommodation, so before you use the agency you should find out how much this charge is likely to be.

Sometimes agencies will ask that parents guarantee the rent. But before signing any agreement you should make sure that you are liable only for your child's rent and not for the whole house.

Most universities have an accommodation office that supplies a list of private rented accommodation in the area. It is best to use these rather than letting agencies as accommodation will have been checked by university staff.

Retainers and reduced rents

In popular student areas or if accommodation is in short supply, your child might be asked to pay a retainer to keep the property over the summer. If they do this they must obtain an agreement signed by them and the landlord and get a receipt for any money they pay. This should stop the landlord giving the property to someone else at the beginning of term.

PAYING FOR UTILITIES

In general, if your child chooses to live in a hall of residence the cost of gas, electricity and water is included in their rent. If they choose to live in private rented accommodation some rents will be inclusive of water, gas and electricity, whereas others will not. They should check with the landlord to find out what bills they are expected to pay.

If your child is offered a property in which rents are inclusive of *water bills*, they could be expected to pay an extra £1.15–£1.40 per week. If rents are inclusive of *all bills*, they could be expected to pay an extra £3–£5.50 on top of their weekly rent.

In private rented accommodation where bills are not included, your child may need to budget for gas, electricity and water supplies. These bills will have to be shared equally between all members of the house – if your child is on a strict budget they should be encouraged to share a house with like-minded people as they can all make sure they save energy and reduce costs together.

Also, they should make sure that they pay only for what they have used. As soon as they move into a property they should take a meter reading and inform the relevant utility company. When they leave the property they need to do the same. They should not rely on readings taken by the landlord or by previous tenants.

Most landlords will ask for your address when your child moves into their property. They do this so that if anyone leaves without paying bills, they can pass on your address to the utility company. Your child should choose their housemates carefully because you could be chased for bills left unpaid by other members of the house.

PAYING THE COUNCIL TAX

Generally, anyone who is at least 18 years old and lives as a resident in a property that is their main or sole dwelling is liable to pay council tax. However, some properties occupied by full-time students are exempt from council tax, and some part-time students and other students may be able to apply for council tax benefits or discounts.

Students should *not* have to pay council tax in the following circumstances:

◆ If your child lives in halls of residence or other types of accommodation owned by the university or college.

- ◆ If your child lives in a house occupied solely by full-time students.

If your child lives with other people who are working, the rules are more complex. All full-time students should apply for exemption from paying the council tax which means that their name should not appear on the bill. However, as it is the property that is taxed, your child may have to negotiate with their housemates about how much they should contribute.

If your child lives with one other person who is working they should be able to apply for exemption. This means that the other person should be able to receive a single person discount of 25 per cent. This is useful if you are a single parent and your child lives with you while they are studying.

Council tax rules concerning exemption, discounts and benefits can be complex and if you are in any doubt about your child's liability to pay you should seek advice from your local Citizen's Advice Bureau.

PAYING FOR COURSE MATERIALS AND BOOKS

The number of books and type of course materials required will depend upon the course, the size of the library and the facilities provided by the college or university. All students will need to buy notepads, pens, A4 paper and printing cartridges if they own a printer.

Your child should be encouraged to consult their course details or speak to their course tutor *before* they buy any materials or books, as they may find that they buy items which will not be needed.

Academic books can be expensive, so they need to think about how many they need to buy. They might find it useful to consult their university library website to find out how many books are held and the ratio of books to students, especially for key texts. Also, many items will be cheaper or available second-hand when they arrive at college or university.

Reducing the costs of course materials and books
There are a number of ways in which your child can reduce the costs of course materials and books:

♦ Purchase stationery and course materials from the Students' Union shop. The Students' Union will be a member of NUS Services. This is the commercial arm of the Students' Union movement in the UK. It specialises in collective purchasing arrangements and direct marketing to students.

Through NUS Services special deals are made between Students' Unions and suppliers on all items sold in Union shops. This includes stationery and course materials and your child will find that most items are offered at a cheaper price than they are in high street shops.

♦ Whenever your child buys anything needed for their course from high street shops, they should check to see whether the retailer offers a student discount. They should take their library card or NUS card with them so that they can prove that they are a student. Some bookshops, especially those situated near to a college or university will offer student discounts of up to ten per cent.

◆ Your child should not buy all the books on the reading list. They should find out which books are the key texts and how many copies are available in the university library. If they want to buy a key text they should consider buying a second-hand copy. Some Students' Union shops or university bookshops buy and sell second-hand books. Also second-hand books can be found on student notice-boards and auction websites.

PAYING FOR IT EQUIPMENT

If your child is on a budget, they do not need to buy any IT equipment while they are at college or university as all their IT requirements can be met by the learning provider. The equipment is free to use and is upgraded constantly, enabling them to use the latest technology without any cost.

They will be given an account on the central system which enables them to access the internet, prepare assignments, use the latest software and send and receive email.

However, many students find that they are more comfortable using their own PC and printer in their room. If this is the case they need to work out how much they can afford to spend on computing equipment. Also, they should decide exactly what they need from a computer and not install more software than they need. Prices vary enormously and your child should be encouraged to shop around for the best deals.

Choosing IT equipment

Many universities have a computer shop in which computing equipment can be purchased at educational prices. Generally, a wide range of specialist and commercial packages are available and staff will be able to offer useful advice. Other suppliers are also able to offer equipment at educational prices. Your child will need to prove that they are a student when receiving this type of discount.

Each year a large amount of university IT equipment is taken out of service. Some universities have a disposal procedure under which equipment is sanitised to make it available for re-sale to students. Supplies may be limited so your child will need to contact the *computer services department* as soon as possible to find out what is available.

Many students advertise second-hand equipment when they decide to upgrade or when they leave university. Your child should check university notice-boards, student newsletters and student auction websites for more information. Second-hand computing equipment can be bought very cheaply and many students find that it is adequate for their three years of study.

PAYING FOR PHOTOCOPYING AND LASER PRINTING

Photocopying costs vary between institutions. In general your child should expect to pay 5p–7p for black and white A4 and 50p–60p for colour A4. Some colleges and universities offer a number of free credits at the beginning of a course. Your child can reduce costs by photocopying only that which is really necessary.

Most tutors request that all coursework is word-processed and presented neatly on one side of A4 paper. If your child does not own a personal computer and printer they will need to use college or university equipment and pay each time they use their printers, although some institutions provide a free or cheaper printing service for draft copies.

As with photocopying, laser printing costs vary between institutions. In general, your child could expect to pay 5p–8p for black and white A4 and 20p–50p for colour A4. Again, some institutions provide a number of free credits at the start of the course and costs can be reduced by printing only what is necessary.

PAYING FOR INSURANCE

Most universities recommend that students take out insurance. It is useful for your child to obtain insurance which covers against theft and accidental damage.

The price of insurance will depend upon the value of your child's possessions, the area in which they are studying, the number and value of additional premiums they choose to pay and the insurance company they decide to use.

The cheapest annual policies start at about £30, although these can be quite difficult to obtain. The most expensive policies, which include additional premiums, may cost up to £170 a year.

Policies vary between companies and your child will need to check carefully that their insurance gives them the level of cover they require. However, as a general guide they may be offered cover for the following:

- **Room contents** – this cover is suitable for all the possessions your child keeps at their term-time address. The insurance should protect against theft (including open door walk-ins), burst pipes, fire, storm, vandalism and flood while in their room. It may also cover their possessions while in your home during the vacations or during direct transit to and from your home.

- **Landlord's property** – some companies will offer this cover as part of the policy. This tends to be against loss or damage of property.

- **Items they regularly take from their room** – for an additional premium they can insure items such as watches, glasses, personal stereos, jewellery and jackets against accidental damage or loss anywhere in the UK. Bikes must be insured separately.

- **Computer cover** – for an additional premium they can insure all items of computer equipment against theft, loss or damage anywhere in the UK.

- **Extra vacation cover** – if your child is going to leave their property over the vacation they can take out additional cover which will insure their possessions against theft while they are away. This cover may be provided free if they live in halls of residence.

- **Mobile phones** – for an additional premium (which can be quite hefty) your child can insure their mobile phone against theft, damage and airtime abuse.

- **Accidental damage** – for an additional premium they can cover electrical equipment in their room.

- **College property on loan** – some policies will cover your child for items of college or university property that are lost or damaged while in their possession, such as books or electrical equipment.

Before your child buys insurance, they should check whether your insurance can be extended to cover them while they are away. Some home contents insurance policies will cover a member of the family when they are living away and this will include students. Also, your child should only buy the cover they need and should not be persuaded to take out more than this by sales people on commission.

PAYING FOR TRAVEL

Travel can use up a large part of the student budget. However, the amount your child spends on travel will depend upon a number of factors:

- How close they live to your home.
- How often they decide to return home.
- How close they live to college or university.
- The part of the country in which they choose to study.
- The cost of public transport and/or petrol in their chosen location.

It is not possible to say how much your child will spend on travel as all the above factors have to be taken into account. However, running a car is usually the most expensive option and most students find that it is cheaper not to run a car while at college or university.

Although train travel is often more expensive than coach travel, sometimes it is easier and more convenient for students to travel by train. If this is the case your child should invest in a Young Person's Railcard. This is available for anyone between the ages of 16 and 25 and entitles them to a third off most rail journeys.

If coach travel is more convenient, your child should purchase a National Express Student Discount Coach-card. This is available to any full-time student and enables them to save up to 30 per cent on the normal adult fare. Many universities and colleges have their own coach stop on campus and National Express serves over 1,200 destinations in the UK.

USEFUL INFORMATION

Useful addresses

Further details about student accommodation, council tax, travel and budgeting can be obtained from the National Union of Students:
NUS
461 Holloway Road
London N7 6LJ
Tel: 020 7272 8900
Website: www.nusonline.co.uk

Uniaid is a registered charity that offers accommodation bursaries for students who are struggling financially. More information can be obtained from:
Uniaid Foundation
The Tower Building
12th Floor
11 York Road

London SE1 7NX
Tel: 020 7922 1699
Website: www.uniaid.org.uk

Useful websites

www.nussl.co.uk
This website provides more information about NUS Services.

www.books4beer.com
www.abebooks.co.uk
www.ebay.co.uk
Second-hand books can be obtained from these sites.

www.endsleigh.co.uk
This is the biggest insurer of student possessions. Many universities have a branch on or close to campus, or Endsleigh will be listed in your local telephone directory. Your child can obtain an online, hassle-free quotation.

www.statravel.co.uk.
STA Travel specialises in travel for students and young people and many universities have a branch on campus. Consult their website for more information.

www.youngpersons-railcard.co.uk
More information about the Young Person's Railcard can be obtained from this website.

Useful publications

I have written a book called *Financial Survival for Students* which deals with issues of student income, expenditure and money management in more depth. For more information consult www.studentcash.org.uk.

You may find the following books useful:

Boehm, K. and Lees-Spalding, J. (2005) *The Student Book, 2006*, 27th edition, Trotman.

Thomas, G. (2005) St*udents' Money Matters, 2005*, 11th edition. Trotman.

7

Helping with Learning Choices

As a parent you may be keen to help your child with their learning choices to ensure that the right ones are made. However, in my research with parents it was found that one of the main causes of argument within families was alternative views about what constitutes a 'suitable' choice, as the following quotation reveals:

> Talk about arguments. I'd been to Nottingham University and I wanted my daughter to go there. I enjoyed it and I knew she would, and it was close to home. But she was sure she wanted to go to Bristol. I don't think the course was so good and the staff we talked too just didn't seem the same. She just wouldn't listen to reason. I'm still not happy about it. It's caused quite a bit of friction really.
>
> Rosalind, 44

Some young people have very definite ideas of what and where they want to study. They may not be open to suggestions and alternative choices. Others have very little idea about their choices and may be more willing to discuss the different options.

In both cases it is important to provide your child with the opportunity to find out what options are available and discuss choices rationally and logically without argument.

This chapter provides advice on obtaining information, using advice services, using league tables, avoiding arguments, reaching consensus and enabling effective decision-making.

OBTAINING INFORMATION

When you are helping your child to think about their learning choices it is useful to obtain as much information as possible so that they can make an informed choice.

Your child's school or the local library should hold prospectuses from most colleges and universities in the country, or you can visit individual websites or order prospectuses direct from the learning provider.

Details of colleges and universities within the UK can be obtained from www.ecctis.co.uk and www.ucas.ac.uk. More information about learning opportunities can be obtained from the Learning and Skills Council or the Department for Education and Skills. If you live in Northern Ireland you can obtain more information from the Department for Employment and Learning (full details below).

Connexions Partnerships provide guidance for 13–19 year olds. Each school has at least one Connexions personal adviser who can give impartial advice on future learning and employment opportunities. They work closely with schools and colleges to ensure that the needs of young people are met. More information can be obtained from www.connexions.gov.uk.

USING ADVICE AND GUIDANCE SERVICES

Advice on further learning opportunities is offered to all Year 9 pupils by school staff. In addition to this advice, some Year 9 pupils may receive advice from a Connexions personal adviser. This tends to be for pupils with statements of special needs or pupils who have been referred to a Connexions adviser by their school. This is useful for students who are interested in following a strongly vocational route.

In Years 10 and 11 all students receive further advice and guidance from school staff and many will receive guidance from the Connexions adviser.

By Year 11 all pupils should have received the following advice:

♦ Careers education programmes.
♦ Information on the full range of options available.
♦ Information on where they might study.
♦ Practical examples and visits.
♦ Information on possible progression routes.
♦ Impartial and challenging guidance.
♦ Information about the financial support available.

In addition to this advice offered through your child's school you can seek advice from other organisations. Your local further education college will have an adviser experienced in working with young people. All universities have an information, advice and guidance (IAG) service where you can obtain more information about the courses on offer.

If you seek information from a specific learning provider, however, you should note that most will recommend courses at their institution. If your child needs more general advice, they should use their local Connexions service.

USING LEAGUE TABLES

League tables are becoming increasingly popular as a method for helping choose a learning provider. However, the position of a college or university in a league table should not be the main reason for persuading your child to study at a particular place.

Your child needs to be happy with their studies and the place of study. This will help them to remain motivated and succeed on the course. If they are pushed into studying an inappropriate course at a place they do not like, they are less likely to do well or enjoy their studies.

Going to college and university is a whole new life experience. In addition to helping young people to prepare for employment and their future life, further education should be enjoyed, valued and remembered for years to come. League tables cannot show the personal, social and cultural advantages gained by each student studying at a particular college or university. In my opinion, league tables should be treated with caution.

However, if you are interested in looking at university rankings, the *Ultimate University Ranking Guide* is a useful book. It pulls together all the different ranking tables and lists them in one comprehensive resource. It is published by Trotman and should be available in your local library.

ATTENDING OPEN DAYS

Once your child has started to narrow down their choices you can visit the learning providers in which they are interested. Most will hold open days for students and parents to visit the site and speak to staff. Dates will be advertised on websites and in prospectuses. Some institutions will request that you book a place for specific tours.

Although the content and structure of open days will vary, in general you should be offered the following:

- An introduction to the college or university.
- Subject talks.
- Tours of the library and IT facilities.
- Campus tours with current students.
- Accommodation tours.
- Visits to the welfare, social and sports facilities.

Your child may find it helpful to design a checklist before you make your visit. If they fill this in on the day it will help them to remember the specific points about each college or university. This will help them to make their final decisions.

You may find it useful to obtain the booklet *The Student's Choice* which helps your child to record and timetable their research when choosing a university or college. If your child's school subscribes to ECCTIS, this publication is available for £1 per copy. It can be ordered from enquiries@ecctis.co.uk or by telephoning 01242 252627.

REACHING CONSENSUS AND AVOIDING ARGUMENTS

Some young people are unsure about their future learning and career goals and it can be useful to help them to understand the opportunities available. You should view your role as a significant adult as opening doors, rather than closing them – helping them to make choices rather than telling them what to do.

You know the importance of listening to your child. Begin by working your way through the four 'Ws'. Ask your child the following questions and listen to their answers without comment or judgement.

◆ What do you want to study?
◆ Where do you want to study?
◆ Why do you want to study this subject?
◆ When do you want to begin your course?

From their answers you will be able to understand the importance of their choices and decisions. If they can answer all questions fully, without hesitation and with enthusiasm, and you agree with their choices, consensus is reached and arguments avoided!

However, in most cases life is not that simple. Some young people do not know what they want to study. Some parents may have a very good idea of what their child *should* study which is different to that which *interests* their child.

It is important not to force, bully or cajole your child into studying something which does not interest them as it will

be hard for them to remain motivated through the course
and their work will suffer as a consequence.

ENCOURAGING EFFECTIVE DECISIONS

If your child is finding it hard to make decisions you need
to help them work through the options in a non-
judgemental, non-forceful way. By asking your child to
work through the following questions, you will help them
to think more about their choices.

The subject

1. What is your favourite subject at school? Why do you
   like this subject?

2. Would you be happy continuing with this subject, or
   would you prefer to study something else?

3. What other subjects interest you? Why?

4. Do you prefer to study just one subject in considerable
   depth, or do you prefer to study a variety of subjects?

5. Are there any subjects you really do not like? Why do
   you not like the subject? (Remember that if it is to do
   with the teacher or teaching methods, these will change
   at college or university.)

6. Do you enjoy learning new subjects? Are you confident
   to tackle new subjects?

The level

1. Are you likely to obtain the qualifications necessary to
   get a place on the course?

2. Do your teachers think you would be able to do well on the course?

3. What are the work requirements? Will you be able to complete all the work required?

4. How much independent work will you need to complete? Are you able to work well using your own initiative?

5. What standard and level of work are required?

The structure

1. For how long would you like to continue studying? Is the course the right length for you?

2. Is the course structured in a way that would suit your learning style?

3. How many classes are you expected to attend? Will you be able to do this?

4. Is the course designed around two semesters or the more traditional three terms? Does this suit you?

5. Does the course run on a modular basis? What modules are available? Are you happy with the selection?

The teaching methods

1. What are your favourite teaching methods at school? Why are they your favourite?

2. What will be the teaching methods on your course? Do they match your preferences?

3. Do you like independent study? How much independent study is required?

4. Do you like working in groups? How much group-work is required?

5. Do you like taking examinations? Is the course examined?

6. Are you familiar with your learning style? Would the course suit this style? (There are a variety of interactive quizzes on the internet which will help you to think more about your learning style.)

The location
1. Do you want to live at home or away from home?

2. How much travel are you willing to undertake? Can you afford to do so? Is the institution well served by public transport, or, if you have a car, is there enough free car-parking available?

3. Would you prefer a campus setting or a place in the heart of the city?

4. Do you want to live in a large city or a smaller town?

5. Have you considered other countries in the UK? (Top-up fees up to £3,000 are only to be introduced in England and Northern Ireland in 2006/07 – would this influence your decision?)

The facilities
1. Would you like to live in student halls of residence? If so, is there enough accommodation available? Are you likely to be successful in acquiring accommodation? Is the cost of accommodation within your budget?

2. What learning facilities are available? Is the library well resourced?

3. What information technology is available?

4. What social facilities are available? Would you prefer a thriving entertainment scene or something a little quieter?

5. How successful is the Students' Union at arranging promotions, discounts, campaigns and entertainment? Is this important to you?

6. What sporting facilities are available?

7. What student support facilities are available, such as medical centres, religious services, counselling and welfare? Is it adequate for your needs?

Financial considerations

1. Can you afford to study away from home? How much would it cost to travel home?

2. Are there part-time employment opportunities available in your chosen location? Does the learning provider run an employment service for students?

3. Will you be able to receive financial help from the government or from other sources?

4. How much are tuition fees? Will you be able to receive help with tuition fees?

5. What bursaries are available from the learning provider? Do you qualify for a bursary?

Future prospects:

1. Are you hoping to gain employment after your studies? If so, how well will your course prepare you for employment?

2. Will you have the opportunity to gain skills relevant to employment while you are studying?

3. Are there employment/voluntary work opportunities available?

4. How well will you be prepared for independent living?

5. Will the course provide the opportunity for personal growth and fulfilment?

USEFUL INFORMATION

Useful addresses

The Learning and Skills Council (LSC) was established in April 2001, replacing the Training and Enterprise Councils and the Further Education Funding Council. The LSC is divided into local councils which can offer information and advice about what is happening in your region. To find out the address and telephone of your local Learning and Skills Council contact:

Learning and Skills Council

Cheylesmore House

Quinton Road

Coventry CV1 2WT

General enquiries helpline: 0870 900 6800

Website: www.lsc.gov.uk (this site provides contact details for all local Learning and Skills Councils).

The Department for Education and Skills (DfES) provides information on many aspects of education and learning opportunities. It has a comprehensive website that covers issues of student learning and funding. It also produces a number of booklets for prospective students. Write for more information or consult their website:

Department for Education and Skills

Sanctuary Buildings

Great Smith Street

London SW1P 3BT

Website: www.dfes.gov.uk

If you live in Northern Ireland contact the Department for Employment and Learning for more information:

Department for Employment and Learning

Adelaide House

39-49 Adelaide Street

Belfast

BT2 8FD

Tel. 028 9025 7728

Website: www.delni.gov.uk

Useful websites

www.ecctis.co.uk

A detailed description of every university and college in the UK is included on this site along with details of British qualifications that can be obtained in further and higher education. A booklet called *The Student's Choice* is available from this site. The booklet is designed to help your child record and timetable their research when choosing a university or college.

www.ucas.ac.uk

The Universities and Colleges Admissions Service (UCAS) is the organisation through which students make their application to university. On their website you can access details of colleges and universities throughout the UK. Each listing contains a link to the college or university website, contact details, information about open days and interviews, accommodation type and cost, overseas study opportunities, subjects and student numbers.

From this website you can order a copy of *The Big Guide – 2005 Entry*. This provides details about qualifications needed for entry into higher education, details about the UCAS Tariff and university data. However, the book is expensive – so check whether it is available in your local library or child's school.

www.hotcourses.com

This site contains detailed listings of colleges and universities, along with information about student finance, choosing a course and finding out about different careers. The following publications are available from this site:

The Hotcourses Student Money Directory
The Hotcourses University and College Guide
The Hotcourses UK Universities, Colleges and Schools Handbook

www.crac.org.uk

This organisation produces the CRAC Degree Course Guides. Twenty guides are available, each covering a different discipline. The guides include information on subjects, courses, admission requirements and work and career opportunities.

www.careerswales.com

Careers Wales Online provides careers related information and advice for all age groups. The website contains a section on learning choices which enables your child to find a suitable course anywhere in Wales.

www.careers-scotland.org.uk
Careers Scotland provides a starting point for anyone looking for careers information, advice and guidance. The website includes information about learning choices and financial help for students who wish to study in Scotland.

www.learndirect-advice.co.uk
The learndirect course database contains details of learning opportunities throughout the UK and can be accessed through this site. Learndirect can also be contacted by telephone: 0800 100 900 (England) and 0808 100 9000 (Scotland).

www.aimhigher.ac.uk
The Aimhigher website has been created to provide information for people interested in entering higher education in the UK. Through this website your child can compare careers, profile a profession, match qualifications to degree types and choose a suitable course.

Useful publications

To find out what courses are available at further education level in the UK, consult the following books, which should be available in your local library, local careers service, Connexions or your child's school library:

Directory of Further Education: The Complete Guide to over 70,000 Further Education Courses in the UK (2004). Hobsons.
Directory of UK Universities, Colleges and Schools (2004). Hobsons.
Financial Times (2004) *Directory of Vocational and Further Education*. Prentice Hall.

To help your child with their higher education choices, you may find some of these books useful:

Catherine Harris (2004) *Ultimate University Ranking Guide.* Trotman.

CRAC (2003) *Directory of Higher Education.* Hobsons.

Brian Heap (2004) *Choosing your Degree Course and University.* Trotman.

Piers Dudgeon (2004) *The Virgin Alternative Guide to British Universities.* Virgin Books.

Piers Dudgeon (2004) *The Virgin Guide to Courses for Careers: Choosing the Right Degree for your Ideal Job.* Virgin Books.

Jimmy Leach (editor) (2004) *The Guardian University Guide: What to Study, Where to Study and How to Make Sure You Get There.* Atlantic Books.

Johnny Rich (2004) *The Push Guide to Choosing a University.* Nelson Thornes.

Andrew Hindmarsh et. al. (2004) *The Times Good University Guide.* Collins.

Kara Fitzhugh (2004) *The Virgin University Survival Guide.* Virgin Books.

8

Finding Special Needs/ Disability Provision

Many parents find that it is an anxious and nerve-wracking time when their children decide to go away to college or university. This is particularly so for parents of children with special needs, as Jane illustrates in the example below:

> As a parent of a year 11 boy who I hope will go to university, I have many questions and anxieties, not least because he has special needs in the form of Asperger's Syndrome/ADD symptoms, nor do I know of anybody in my immediate family who has been to university.
>
> My worries would concern the practical issues of housekeeping, timekeeping and keeping up with the workload as well as his pastoral needs. Other concerns would be that if an assignment was not completed or handed in on time, how he would be penalised. Who could keep an eye out for my son if or when he got into financial difficulties, aside from the fact that most students leave uni with thousands of pounds of debt?
>
> Jane

In my research many parents, like Jane, were concerned about the availability of pastoral support, financial support and learner support facilities. They wanted to know how they could find more information and secure a suitable place with all the necessary support for their child, whatever their special needs.

This chapter provides information for parents of children with disabilities and special needs, covering issues such as learner support, equipment and facilities, help with mobility and obtaining financial support.

KNOWING YOUR CHILD'S RIGHTS

Learning providers need to comply with the Special Educational Needs and Disability Act (SENDA) 2001, which is an amendment to the Disability Discrimination Act (DDA) 1995. This Act states that there should be no discrimination on the grounds of disability.

Under this Act learning providers must make reasonable adjustments so that disabled students are not at an unreasonable disadvantage compared to students who are not disabled.

In their equal opportunities policies learning providers point out that they are committed to promoting access for students who have a disability, dyslexia and/or long-term medical condition. Entry for places is based on academic merit and your child's disability should not influence recruitment decisions.

Some of the bigger colleges and universities have a special office or department that deals with disability issues. Details of these offices can be obtained from university websites or prospectuses. Support and facilities will vary, but institutions should have accessible rooms, specialist equipment, note-takers, advisers and support workers. They should also be willing to make special examination arrangements if required (see below).

UNDERSTANDING THE ROLE OF DISABILITY OFFICERS AND ADVISERS

The role of the disability officer or adviser is to ensure that students with disabilities receive all the help and support they need to succeed in their studies.

The disability adviser can help your child with their application for Disabled Students' Allowances (DSA). These are funds set up by the government to help with extra costs your child may have to pay as a result of their disability (see below).

Disability advisers will arrange an appointment for an assessment of needs which is required for your child's DSA application. Some of the larger institutions will have a recognised Assessment Centre on campus.

The disability adviser will help your child to arrange suitable accommodation while at college or university – if they need extra equipment, such as a fridge to store medicine, this will be arranged. Also, they will liaise on your child's behalf with staff about other special arrangements, such as help with examinations, study skills and transport to and from college and within the campus.

FINDING SUITABLE ACCOMMODATION

University and college accommodation varies considerably. However, suitable living accommodation for people with disabilities should be available. When your child makes their application they should make contact with the disability adviser as soon as possible. This person will arrange for you and your child to meet with the accommodation officer to discuss your child's requirements. Every effort will be made to meet their needs.

Accommodation in halls of residence may be available for the whole course if your child has special requirements. However, your child must apply as soon as possible as this type of accommodation may be limited.

Catered halls will provide meals for students on special diets, but again your child needs to discuss their needs as soon as possible so that arrangements can be put into place.

OBTAINING HELP WITH MOBILITY

Some colleges and universities provide a minibus service for people who have mobility difficulties. This is available to help your child to move between campuses and buildings so that they can attend lectures and visit the library. If a minibus service is not available, some institutions will provide a taxi at no cost to the student.

Your child needs to discuss their requirements at the beginning of term and provide a copy of their timetable so that routes can be organised. Contact the university or college to find out if such a service is available.

OBTAINING SUPPORT WITH LEARNING RESOURCES

Library staff within most colleges and universities will provide a personal tour for people with disabilities so that they can assess your child's needs and any potential problems.

Some libraries will provide staff who can offer one-to-one support throughout your child's course. Depending upon the funds available, specialist equipment offered by the library may include the items listed below:

- a PC with a large monitor, scanner and screen-reading software
- speech synthesiser facilities for IT
- amplifiers
- hearing loop systems
- publications and instructions in Braille.

OBTAINING STUDY SUPPORT

Most institutions have a *Study Support Centre* or *Academic Support Unit*. These provide extra support for students with study difficulties (see Chapter 11). Details of these units can be obtained from websites or prospectuses.

In these units trained members of staff are able to offer one-to-one support for your child. They will be able to liaise with your child's course tutor and negotiate special arrangements for completing work and handing in assignments if your child has a recognised medical condition. They will also be able to offer support and liaise with tutors if your child struggles to meet deadlines.

Some institutions train students to become note-takers. These students will attend lectures with your child and take notes if they have problems hearing or writing.

The disability officer will be able to help to arrange for lip readers or signers to attend lectures if they are required and will also make arrangements for your child to be accompanied by guide dogs or hearing dogs. They will be able to make sure that hearing loop systems are in place for lectures, if required.

ARRANGING EXAMINATION SUPPORT

Your child's disability adviser will be able to help them make alternative examination arrangements. These depend upon your child's requirements and may include the arrangements listed below:

- Additional time and extra reading time.
- Rest breaks.
- Flexible starting time.
- Personal assistance, such as a scribe, reader or interpreter.
- Specialist equipment, such as computers, dictionaries and furniture.
- Large print, Braille or audio-tape exam papers.
- A separate venue.

All students will be required to provide written medical evidence if they wish to have special arrangements put in place. The disability officer will be able to provide information about the type of evidence required.

OBTAINING FINANCIAL SUPPORT

The Disabled Students' Allowances (DSAs) are funds set up by the government to help with extra costs your child may have to pay as a result of their disability. The funds will pay for non-medical personal help, major items of specialist equipment, travel and other course-related costs. Funds depend on need, not on your family income.

Students with disabilities are eligible to apply for all other forms of government funding, such as help with tuition fees, student loans, higher education grants and Access to Learning Funds.

DSAs are available for students who are intending to study either full-time or part-time within the higher education sector. Undergraduates, postgraduates, Open University students and distance learners are eligible to apply for the funds. DSAs are available for students studying in all parts of the UK.

Levels of funding

Funds are available to help students with a high level of need. Maximum amounts are available, but most students will not receive the full amount unless they have a high level of need. In 2005/06 the maximum amounts students on *full-time*, undergraduate courses can receive are as follows:

◆ Specialist equipment allowance – up to £4,680 for the whole of your child's course.
◆ Non-medical helper's allowance – up to £11,840 a year.
◆ General Disabled Students' Allowance – up to £1,565 a year.
◆ Reasonable travel expenses.

APPLYING FOR THE DISABLED STUDENTS' ALLOWANCES

Applications for DSAs are made through your LEA or online (England and Wales), ELB (Northern Ireland) and SAAS (Scotland). Your child will need to apply for government financial support following the procedure outlined in Chapter 4.

Applications can be made before the start of your child's course, even if they have not received confirmation of a place. This will ensure that payments are made promptly and ready for the start of the academic year. However, your child can apply for DSAs at any time during their course.

Once the form has been processed your child will receive confirmation of their entitlement to DSAs. If your child's application is turned down you should find out why and if you disagree with the assessment, you are entitled to appeal against the decision.

Many LEAs employ a named officer who deals specifically with applications for DSAs. If there is such a person within your LEA, contact them for advice and guidance. They will be able to help with the application procedure.

UNDERTAKING A NEEDS ASSESSMENT

If your child is entitled to financial help your LEA will ask for a needs assessment to be carried out to find out what kind of help your child needs. Some universities have a recognised Assessment Centre on campus.

Once this needs assessment has been completed your LEA will arrange suitable assistance while your child is studying on their course.

USEFUL INFORMATION

Useful addresses

For more information about any aspect of financial support for students with disabilities, contact:

Student Finance Delivery Division

2F – Area C

Mowden Hall

Staindrop Road

Darlington DL3 9BG

Tel: 01325 392822

Website: www.dfes.gov.uk/studentsupport

A booklet called *Bridging the Gap: a guide to the Disabled Students' Allowances (DSAs)* in higher education can be obtained from this address. This booklet is available in Braille and on audiotape. A free textphone service is available on 0800 328 8988.

You may find the following organisations useful:

Adult Dyslexic Organisation

336 Brixton Road

London SW9 7AA

Tel: 020 7924 9559

Website: www.futurenet.co.uk/charity/ado

Royal National Institute of the Blind

105 Judd Street

London WC1H 9NE

Helpline: 0845 766 9999

Fax: 020 7388 2034

Website: www.rnib.org.uk/student

Royal National Institute for Deaf People
19–23 Featherstone Street
London EC1Y 8SL
Tel: 020 7296 8000
Fax: 020 7296 8199
Textphone: 020 7296 8001
Freephone voicephone: 0808 8080123
Freephone textphone: 0808 8089000
Website: www.rnid.org.uk

Useful publications

Skill (2004) *Into Higher Education, 2005*. This guide offers advice and guidance to students with disabilities who wish to enter higher education. It includes information on making applications and obtaining financial support. The book can be obtained from:
Skill: the National Bureau for Students with Disabilities
Chapter House
18–20 Crucifix Lane
London SE1 3JW
Information Service (1.30pm to 4.30pm Monday to Thursday)
Tel: 0800 328 5050
Minicom: 0800 068 2422
Website: www.skill.org.uk

Skill has also published a booklet called *Disabled Students' Allowances* which gives guidance on the evidence LEAs need from applicants. It contains a useful checklist if your child is planning to apply for DSAs.

Your child may find the following book useful:

Caprez, E. (2004) *The Disabled Students' Guide to University, 2005* (3rd edition). Trotman.

9

Helping with Applications

In my research some parents pointed out that they were confused about the application process and procedures. They wanted to be able to help their child but found that the system was complicated and unclear, as the following quotation from Brian illustrates:

> I thought it was important to give my son a hand, but I didn't know how to. And the worse thing was I didn't know how to find the information. In the end I just left him to it. Obviously his school sorted it all out in the end, but I really wanted to help. If I'm honest about it I guess I felt a bit useless really.
>
> Brian, 58

This chapter explains the application process for further and higher education, providing information about enrolment and induction, what to do if expected qualifications aren't obtained, understanding the Clearing System and helping your child to make a successful application.

APPLYING TO A FURTHER EDUCATION COLLEGE

If your child is interested in a particular further education college, they should request an up-to-date prospectus. In the prospectus they will find information about how to enrol for a course. If your child cannot find the right course, the prospectus should contain details about how to contact a trained adviser (see Chapter 7).

Most college prospectuses will contain a 'request form' which enables your child to request further information about a specific course. Your child should be encouraged to read the information carefully and find out whether the course would meet their specific requirements.

The questions provided in Chapter 7 will help you to talk about the important issues. Again, if you or your child has any doubts you should speak to a trained adviser at the college.

When your child requests specific course information, it should clearly state the level of qualifications required. If it does not, or if your child is in any doubt, contact the college to speak to a trained adviser or to the course tutor.

Enrolment

Once your child has found a suitable course they can fill in and return the enrolment form by post or they can attend an enrolment day where they will have the opportunity to speak to course tutors and other students.

Most colleges will enable students to speak to specialist staff who will be able to discuss the options available, including tailor-made courses and flexible provision.

Once your child has received their exam results the college may contact them again to discuss their results and the options they have chosen to check whether the choices are still suitable.

If your child doesn't do as well as they have expected in their examinations, they should be encouraged to contact the college as soon as possible. A trained adviser will be able to talk through their options and suggest alternative courses. Your child may also find it useful to speak to their school careers tutor or the personal adviser at their local Connexions service.

Induction

Before the course starts, many colleges will run an induction day. This is designed to help your child familiarise themselves with the college and facilities before they start their course. It is useful for your child to attend the induction day as they will be shown helpful services and facilities, including the library and computing facilities.

Although parents may attend the enrolment session, most induction sessions are attended only by students. This enables students to spend some time getting to know other students and staff.

APPLYING TO UNIVERSITY

If your child wants to apply for a full-time, undergraduate course in the UK, they have to make their application through the Universities and Colleges Admissions Service (UCAS). This applies to *all* full-time undergraduate courses, whether they are delivered at universities, colleges of higher education or colleges of further education. UCAS does not deal with applications for part-time courses.

There are two ways to apply through UCAS – the electronic method or the postal method.

◆ **Electronic method** – to make an electronic application your child should apply via a registered school, college, careers or Connexions office. The secure, web-based application system is known as *apply* and most students now make their application using this method. A step-by-step guide called *How to Apply* is available as a help function, clearly guiding your child through each stage of the application process.

◆ **Postal method** – UCAS application forms and the *How to Apply* booklet can be obtained from your child's school, college or Connexions service. Alternatively, your child can request a form from app.req@ucas.ac.uk. For general information about the application process you can telephone 0870 11 222 11 or email enquiries@ucas.ac.uk.

On the application form your child is able to enter up to six choices of university. They can apply to the same university for different courses, but if the content varies significantly between these courses they will be asked to explain their choices.

UNDERSTANDING ENTRY REQUIREMENTS

The UCAS Tariff is a point score system that is used as a way of setting out the entry requirements for the different courses at higher education level. Qualifications that your child receives after post-compulsory schooling are given a points value, and, for the purpose of entry into higher education, these points are added together to find out whether your child meets the entry requirements.

Examples of these points values are provided below:

- ◆ one A Level at grade A = 120 points
- ◆ one AS Level at grade A = 60 points
- ◆ a Vocational Certificate of Education (VCE) double award at grade AA = 240 points

Not all higher education institutions use the points system and others may qualify a points offer by asking for particular subjects or grades.

Your child's school or Connexions service should hold a copy of *The Big Guide – 2005 Entry.* This gives comprehensive details about the entry requirements for each course. Full details of approved qualifications and their tariff points can be obtained from the UCAS websites (details below).

Alternatively, your child can use the *course search* facility on the UCAS website. This enables them to view the university or college entry requirements. Some institutions also provide *entry profiles* which give more detailed information on the courses, entry requirements and selection criteria.

Returning the application form
If your child is applying through their school or college the application forms are given to a staff member who has responsibility for making sure that references are completed and the form returned to UCAS.

If your child is applying to UCAS as an individual, the application form should be returned to:
UCAS
PO Box 67
Cheltenham
Gloucestershire GL52 3ZD.

Your child is required to pay a fee for their application. If they are applying for only one course at one university, the fee is £5. If they are applying to more than one university the fee is £15. All students have to pay these fees, regardless of their personal financial situation. Payment can be arranged through your child's school.

Enrolment and induction

During the summer detailed enrolment and induction guidelines will be sent to any student who has received an unconditional offer. This will provide details of where and when to enrol, information about tuition fees and when to pay them, accommodation details and any other information deemed to be relevant.

Students who have received a conditional offer will be forwarded this information as soon as they have met the terms of their offer.

UNDERSTANDING THE CLEARING SYSTEM

Clearing is run by UCAS and is the system through which students without a higher education place find suitable vacancies on a course. Your child can go through the Clearing System if one of the following applies:

- They declined their offers.
- Their offers have not been confirmed because they have not met the conditions.
- They hold no offers and have not withdrawn from the UCAS scheme.
- They have applied after 30 June.

University courses that still have vacancies after students who have received the required grades have accepted a place are advertised in the national press from the middle of August to late September.

If your child is eligible to go through the Clearing System they will automatically be sent a Clearing Entry Form and instruction leaflet. It is important to note that they will have to deal directly with admissions tutors at this time, so you will need to make sure that your child is available to do this. Admissions tutors will want to speak to the potential entrant and not to parents.

MAKING EFFECTIVE APPLICATIONS

Your child will increase their chances of success if they follow the guidelines set out below. These rules apply to both paper and online applications.

- **Step 1** – they should obtain an application form in good time so that they do not have to rush their application. School or college staff should make appropriate arrangements. Most UCAS applications are filled in from September the year before the course begins, but research should begin before this time, especially if you are wishing to make visits to all the universities in which your child is interested.

- **Step 2** – they should read all instructions and guidelines before they fill in the form. If they do not understand anything, they should seek advice from a trained adviser or school teacher. Any mistakes or omissions will delay their application and may lead to an unfavourable response from admissions staff.

- **Step 3** – it is useful to obtain two application forms or photocopy the form if your child is filling in a paper application. Using the copy, your child can practise filling in the form. They should think through each answer and know what they intend to enter for each section, avoiding repetition and waffle. You can read their draft and check for mistakes.

- **Step 4** – the application form should be completed clearly and neatly and should be free from grammatical errors and spelling mistakes. Your child needs to show that they have undertaken careful and detailed research, both in their personal statement and through their choice of institution and course. If your child is entering up to six courses on a UCAS form, they should not be significantly different from each other as this suggests indecision and lack of research.

- **Step 5** – your child should stress their achievements and market themselves in a positive way. They should show that they are confident, keen and intend to do well on their course. All work experience and extra courses attended should be included, especially if they help to demonstrate motivation and commitment. Your child should think about the skills they possess and relate them to the subject they want to study. Extra curricula activities are valued but should not dominate the form.

- **Step 6** – your child may find it useful to photocopy or print a copy of the completed form so that they have a record of what they have included. This is useful if they are invited for interview.

◆ **Step 7** – it is important that your child familiarise themselves with all closing dates and make sure they post applications in good time, allowing for delays with the postal system. UCAS closing dates are clearly displayed on their website and on application forms – most forms are returned in November. Closing dates for further education courses will be displayed on application forms and within the course material.

USEFUL INFORMATION

Useful addresses

UCAS produces a variety of publications for students making applications. Details of these can be obtained from their website or by contacting:

UCAS Distribution Team
PO Box 130
Cheltenham
Gloucestershire GL52 3ZF
Tel: 01242 544610
Fax: 01242 544960
Email: distribution@ucas.ac.uk

Useful websites

www.ucas.ac.uk
This is the UCAS website which contains information on the application process, points tariff, deadlines and useful publications, some of which are provided as free downloadable guides.

Useful publications

Senior, M. and Mannix, P. (2001) *Writing an Effective Personal Statement.* Senior Press. This book should be available at your child's school or college and is essential reading for those completing their UCAS forms. It includes activities to help your child write their personal statement and contains a tutorial booklet.

Brown, R. and Chant, M. (2003) *Getting In, Getting On!* This book is published by Connexions Somerset and is a useful guide for getting into higher education. It contains exercises and activities designed to prepare your child for the UCAS process and to give your child a better idea of how the selection process works.

Your child may also find this book useful:

Higgins, T. (2004) *How to Complete Your UCAS Form for 2005 Entry.* Trotman.

10

Preparing for College and University

If this is your first child to go away to college or university, it can be difficult to know how to prepare for the move, as Bridget points out:

> I guess it's when it's something new you don't really know what to expect. My son's friends all had their own ideas and they would tell him and then he would tell me. But how do you know? How do you know what they are saying is right? I suspect some of the information I received through these channels was way off the mark. Any good information I can get would be gratefully received.
>
> Bridget

This chapter helps you to prepare for your child going to college or university by providing information on accommodation, course materials, books, computing equipment, field trips and independent living.

MAKING ACCOMMODATION CHOICES

The first question asked by many parents is should my child live in halls of residence or private rented accommodation?

Most students choose to live in halls for their first year away as this provides a safe environment and companionship with many other students. It eases them into college and university life. After the first year when they have made friends they can then decide with whom they would like to live and go house-hunting together.

When your child makes their learning choices they should also think about accommodation. Most learning providers try to provide enough accommodation for all first year students, but sometimes this is not possible. Space may be severely limited so some learning providers operate a first-come-first-served policy. It is important, therefore, that your child applies early if they wish to live in halls of residence.

Using the accommodation office

Most colleges and universities will have an accommodation office. Your child can contact this office as soon as they have been offered a place. Contact details will be provided in the university prospectus or on their website.

Most accommodation offices will provide an information pack to all prospective students. Alternatively, application packs for halls will be sent out with joining instructions.

Keys to halls of residence are allocated through the accommodation office and most will request that a deposit is paid. Checks for damage will be made at the end of term and the deposit will not be returned if the property is damaged.

Many accommodation offices run a landlord registration scheme which means that all registered private rented properties meet specific standards in terms of health and safety and basic standards, such as ensuring that a desk is provided in every room.

Comparing accommodation costs

Many students and parents ask whether it is cheaper to live in halls of residence or private rented accommodation. Unfortunately there is no definitive answer. Some students will find it cheaper to live in halls, whereas others will find it cheaper to live in private rented accommodation. Also, the type, standard and price of accommodation vary enormously between learning providers and between halls (see Chapter 6).

The best way to look at this issue is to decide where your child would like to live and then think about reducing the costs. Your child needs to be happy in their accommodation, so they need to think what would most suit them.

Changing halls of residence

It is important that you and your child visit all accommodation before choosing. Most learning providers ask that students sign an agreement to take up the accommodation for a certain period of time.

If your child decides to move or leaves their course, they may be liable to pay until the end of the agreed time. Many universities also levy an administration charge if your child wishes to change accommodation.

CHOOSING PRIVATE RENTED ACCOMMODATION

If your child wishes to live in private rented accommodation they will need to start looking early, sometimes as soon as January or February before the start of their course. This is one reason why it often easier to consider private rented accommodation in second and third years when students are more familiar with the local area.

Unfortunately, there are a minority of unscrupulous landlords about, and some of them find that new students are easy prey. Your child can reduce the risks by considering the following points when they choose their accommodation:

- Use the university accommodation office. Members of staff inspect property prior to putting it on their list, ensuring that properties conform to health and safety standards. If they receive complaints about landlords, the property will be withdrawn from their list.

- Some universities run a property management service. This means they lease privately owned houses from their owners and let them to students. The university acts as the landlord which serves to protect your child from unscrupulous landlords whilst still giving them their independence.

- Make sure that your child receives a written tenancy agreement signed by them and the landlord. The Students' Union or college welfare officer will be able to offer advice on the agreement.

- Make sure that your child receives receipts for any money they pay, whether deposit or weekly/monthly rent. This will prevent their landlord trying to evict them for rent arrears.

Understanding tenancy agreements

If your child decides to rent privately, they must inspect their tenancy agreement carefully to make sure that their rights are protected.

The Chartered Institute of Environmental Health, with the advice and assistance of the NUS, has produced a comprehensive leaflet called *Safe Housing for Students*. This is available from Students' Unions or from www.nusonline.co.uk. The main points of this leaflet are summarised below:

◆ Is it an individual or joint agreement? If it is an individual agreement your child is responsible only for their share of rent and bills. If it is a joint agreement they will be liable for everybody's rent and bills.

◆ Will your child be sharing the accommodation with the landlord or a member of their family? If so, it might make it easier for the landlord to evict them.

◆ Does the contract state start and finish dates, and clearly state how much rent is to be paid for this time?

◆ Does your child have to pay a deposit? Will a receipt be issued?

◆ Have you seen an up-to-date inventory? Is it correct? This will help to stop the landlord withholding your child's deposit at the end of the tenancy.

◆ Have you been given the landlord's full name and current address? Can your child contact the landlord in an emergency?

- ◆ Have you been asked to pay a retainer to keep the property over the summer? Although this is not illegal, universities and the NUS do not like to encourage this practice.

- ◆ Does the contract state who is responsible for repairs? Landlords are under a statutory duty to keep parts of their property in good repair.

- ◆ Can the landlord provide evidence that all gas appliances have been inspected within the last 12 months? Ask to see a maintenance record.

CHOOSING COURSE MATERIALS AND BOOKS

For most courses your child will be given a reading list, but they do not need to buy all the books on this list. They should check with their tutor to find out which are the key texts, then find out how many copies are available in the university library.

Your child can consider buying second-hand copies if a book is important. These will be advertised on student websites, the college intranet or student notice-boards. Some Students' Union shops or university bookshops buy and sell second-hand books.

The type of course materials required by your child will depend upon their course and the facilities provided by their college or university. However, all students will need to buy notepads, pens, A4 paper and printing cartridges if they own a printer.

Consult the course details or encourage your child to speak to their course tutor *before* buying any materials or books, as they may find the items are not needed. Also, many items will be cheaper or available second-hand when they arrive at college or university.

CHOOSING COMPUTING EQUIPMENT

It is not necessary to buy your child their own IT equipment as all their IT needs can be met by equipment supplied by the learning provider. However, if you feel your child needs their own equipment, remember that educational discounts are available (see Chapter 6).

When choosing software, your child should purchase that which they need to help with their course. In general, this will be because it meets the following criteria:

◆ It is required for their course, or will help with their coursework.
◆ It will save them time.
◆ It will save them money.
◆ It will save them brainwork.

Also, if your child intends to use both their own PC *and* equipment supplied by the learning provider, they will have to make sure that software is compatible.

Some learning providers enable students to access their network from connection points in study bedrooms. If this is the case, your child will need to make sure that their PC is able to run the specific software.

PREPARING FOR FIELD TRIPS

Field trips involve a period of study away from the classroom, led by a tutor, for the purpose of enhancing learning by providing practical examples. This might be a morning trip to a factory or a week-long visit to a place of scientific interest. Field trips can involve travel to all parts of the UK and overseas. Virtual field trips are offered by some universities and colleges if budgets and/or time are restricted.

Some subject areas utilise field trips more than others, for example, if your child is studying geology or geography they can expect to attend at least one field trip each year of their course. However, tutors of other subjects also use field trips to aid learning, so your child should check at the start of the course whether this is the case.

Some learning providers will ask that your child makes a contribution towards the costs, usually to cover accommodation. However, others will include all costs within the course fees.

Buying equipment for field trips

The type of equipment your child needs for field trips will depend on the course, subject and the nature of the field trip. If any part of the field work will be hazardous they will need to wear protective clothing. This could include the items listed below.

◆ safety helmets
◆ eye/face protection
◆ ear defenders

- respiratory protection
- high visibility clothing
- wet suits and life jackets
- aprons
- gloves
- foot protection.

Some of this equipment may be provided by the learning provider, but other items may not. Your child should consult with their tutor about what items may need to be purchased.

For most field trips your child will require the following:

- warm/waterproof clothing
- walking boots or other suitable footwear
- a small rucksack
- a sleeping bag.

PROVIDING EQUIPMENT FOR INDEPENDENT LIVING

In my research with undergraduate students I asked them to list items provided by parents/relatives that had been of most use to them while they lived away from home. Students pointed out that these items did not have to be new – most were second-hand, donated or loaned to them while they were at college or university.

These items appear in the lists below. I have divided the responses between students who live in halls of residence and those who live in private rented accommodation.

Halls of residence

- carpets/rugs
- study lamp
- mugs
- food parcels
- bed linen
- phone card/credits
- towels
- television
- stereo
- small saucepan
- cutlery.

Private rented accommodation

- kettle
- toaster
- crockery
- cutlery
- saucepans
- recipe books
- food parcels
- bedding
- phone card/credits
- iron
- towels
- bicycle
- television
- stereo
- cleaning equipment.

How much you provide for your child will depend on a number of factors:

◆ How much equipment is already provided in the accommodation? You should view all accommodation prior to making arrangements and check what will be included with the accommodation officer or landlord.

◆ How much do you *want* to provide? One of the important parts of going away to college or university is that your child learns to support themselves. If everything is provided for them, how will they learn how to budget and understand the value of material goods?

◆ How secure is their accommodation? If the goods are expensive would they be tempting for burglars? (See Chapter 13.)

◆ If your child has a lot of possessions, how will they transport them between college and your home? Are they able to store their goods somewhere safe and secure during vacations?

◆ How much is provided by other members of the house? There is little point duplicating equipment.

Providing electrical equipment in halls of residence

If your child intends to live in halls of residence they will need to find out what electrical equipment is permissible.

In their rules and regulations, learning providers will state that all electrical equipment must be in safe working order. Particular attention must be paid to the fuse and wiring. Some colleges and universities will ask that an electrical safety certificate is provided with all electrical equipment. Others will request that the equipment be subject to a university safety test.

Some learning providers have a maximum permissible power loading for electrical equipment. All require plugs not to be overloaded and trailing leads are not permitted.

If your child takes their own television, they will need to obtain a TV licence, in both halls of residence and private rented accommodation. TV licence detectors are particularly keen on checking private rented accommodation that has previously been issued with a licence – make sure your child is not caught out as fines are huge.

Forbidden items in halls

Certain items are not allowed in halls of residence. These vary between learning providers, but in general include the following:

- candles
- pets
- faulty electrical equipment
- chip pans/deep fat fryers
- heaters
- additional furniture (this may be allowed, subject to approval).

All halls of residence will have a list of rules and regulations – your child should study these before taking up a place. Most regulations reserve the right for university staff to enter the room at any time – if students are found to be in breach of the rules they may be fined or expelled from the accommodation.

USEFUL INFORMATION

Useful addresses

For more details about special offers on stationery, course materials and books, your child should contact their Students' Union or visit their website. Further details about services offered by the National Union of Students can be obtained from:

NUS

461 Holloway Road

London N7 6LJ

Tel: 020 7272 8900

Website: www.nusonline.co.uk

11

Supporting their Studies

Parents in my research felt that it was important to be able to support their children with their studies. However, as some parents had not been through further and higher education themselves, they felt that this was difficult to do because they did not understand what facilities were available and what was expected of students. Also, as parents, they did not know how much they could become involved in their child's education, as the following quotation illustrates:

> My daughter was ill in her first year. I didn't know what to do, who to ring and speak to about her assignments, like even whether I could actually do that. She couldn't do it, she was just too ill but I didn't know what to do. How much can you be involved? I know she's technically an adult, but she's still my daughter and I want to help as much as possible, like with her work and things like that.
>
> Brenda, 47

This chapter has been written to provide information to parents on the existing support structure available within colleges and universities. It explains what student and learner support is available and provides information on the Data Protection and Freedom of Information Acts. This will help you, as a parent, to understand how and to what extent you can become involved in your child's education.

KNOWING ABOUT LEARNING RESOURCES

All colleges and universities have their own *library* or *learning resource centre* which should contain the learning resources your child needs to successfully complete their course. Resources will vary between institutions, but in general your child should have access to most or all of the facilities listed below:

- text books
- reference books
- short loan and standard loan collection
- inter-library loan
- journals
- exam papers
- archives/databases
- document services
- printing and binding
- self-service copying and laser printing
- fact-sheets and instruction booklets
- video and audio equipment
- microfilm equipment
- equipment for the visually impaired
- access and visitor information
- helpdesk
- training courses on how to use databases and journals.

The library may offer an *Interlending and Document Supply* service which means that your child can access books, journals, maps and documents from other university libraries if they are not available in their library.

Most libraries will have a website that can be accessed by your child before they begin their studies so that they can see what facilities are available. Your child should also be encouraged to take part in the library tour at the beginning of term as this is the best way to find out how to use the services.

The library catalogue

All learning providers will have a computerised library catalogue which will enable your child to search the entire library stock using a variety of search techniques. It will show them in which building the publication is located and let them know whether it is out on loan.

Most catalogues can be accessed from your child's PC if they have access to the university network. They can use the library catalogue to check their own record of loans, self-renew their books and request other books. The self-renewal facility is useful to renew books and avoid fines if, for whatever reason, your child is unable to return the books on time.

If your child has problems travelling to their college, they may be offered a postal service for taking out and returning books.

KNOWING ABOUT LEARNER SUPPORT SERVICES

There are a wide variety of learner support services available for students within most colleges and universities. The tutors and other staff want your child to do well on their course and they will try to provide any extra services that will help them to succeed.

As a student your child is entitled to use any of these services and most will be free of charge. Services may include learner support units, study support sessions, individual workshops and training. If your child believes they are struggling with their studies encourage them to discuss their problems with their tutor, who will be able to offer advice on the best course of action.

Learner support units

Many colleges and universities have a *learner support unit* or *study skills unit* that is available to help students with basic skills in reading, writing and numeracy. If your child is struggling with any of these skills special sessions can be arranged. These are held within the unit and will be arranged to suit your child's course timetable.

In the unit they can access learning resources and materials, computing facilities and other technological aids. Advice from supportive, trained staff is available when required. The aim of these units is to give students the skills and confidence to move on in their studies until they no longer need the support of the unit.

This type of learner support tends to be offered in an informal, workshop setting – your child can either book a regular time to visit or drop into the unit. This can be useful when they need help with something that may be short-term and quite specific.

The learner support tutor

At most institutions your child will have a confidential interview with the learning support tutor who will discuss the problems they are facing, looking at their strengths and weaknesses and their hopes and fears. An individual learning plan will be developed which will lay out your child's aims and objectives, setting realistic goals for the short and long term.

The learner support tutor will focus on information relevant to your child's course which makes the help they receive more interesting, relevant and useful. Some tutors will liaise with your child's course tutor to make sure that they give them the best possible help.

Study support sessions

Many colleges and universities will offer study support sessions for students who would like extra help with study skills such as essay writing, note-taking, presentation skills and revision techniques. A timetable of sessions is drawn up each semester or term.

The sessions are free to students and your child can choose which sessions they wish to attend. They are led by an experienced tutor and time may be set aside at the end of the session for individual students to raise questions.

Training and workshops

Some institutions run extra training and workshops in subjects that may not have direct relevance to your child's course, but which may be of personal interest to them or useful to future careers. This may include sessions in counselling skills, interview techniques, compiling CVs and assertiveness.

Many of these sessions will be free for students, although places are often limited so your child will need to book early. They should contact the *student and staff develop-ment team*, *human resource department* or *student enterprise centre* at their college or university for more information.

KNOWING ABOUT INFORMATION TECHNOLOGY SERVICES

The IT equipment and services available will vary between institutions. However, most university and college computing services will provide some or all of the equipment and services listed below:

- a campus network of PCs, some with 24-hour access
- workstations and laboratories
- advice and help desk service
- printing and binding services
- electronic mail
- network connection service
- audio visual equipment
- remote access services
- file recovery service
- assistance and training in most/all aspects of ICT use
- a computer shop selling hardware and software at educational prices
- sanitised equipment for re-sale to students.

When your child makes their learning choices they should consult college and university prospectuses and websites to find out what equipment will be available for their use. Many *computing services departments* will have their own website and will list the equipment available.

If your child attends an open day they will be shown IT services and the equipment available. They should be encouraged to think about questions that they can ask the tour guide when they are shown around campus.

Once they enrol on their course they can visit the *computing services department* which will be able to provide information about the equipment and services on offer. Many of these departments run training sessions for students unfamiliar with the equipment or software.

Using the internet
All students can access the internet from college or university computers free of charge. However, some learning providers may limit the amount of time students can spend online and others will limit the amount of space students are given to store the information they have down-loaded.

Many college study bedrooms have connection points for linking to the internet and the university network. Guidelines for connecting computers will be provided by IT staff.

Most learning providers will ask that students register the equipment they intend to use in their bedrooms. Although connection may be free, students will have to pay for their time online and will be responsible for making sure all payment is up to date.

All learning providers will have strict rules about obscene material, software theft, breach of copyright and plagiarism. They will also not allow the running of businesses from computers in study bedrooms. A list of rules and regulations can be obtained from the computing services department.

Setting up an email account

Most colleges and universities automatically register new students for their central email system. Different email systems are structured in different ways – when your child registers, they should ask staff how they get started on the system.

Colleges and universities have strict rules and regulations about using email – in most places sending offensive messages or material that belongs to other people is considered a serious offence. Also, your child will not be able to use the college email system for running a business or for any profit-making scheme.

UNDERSTANDING THE DATA PROTECTION ACT

The Data Protection Act 1998 came into force in March 2000 and imposes major responsibilities on colleges and universities to manage and protect the personal data they keep on their students. This applies to written and electronic data.

Members of college and university staff frequently receive requests from parents about their child's progress on their course. However, students are private individuals and the learning provider has no responsibility or legal obligation to keep parents informed of their progress or other aspects of their studies or private lives.

The fact that you may have paid large sums of money for your child's education does not entitle you to this information. Only if your child has given their consent, usually in the form of written consent, will staff pass on the information you require.

Personal information will be disclosed in exceptional circumstances, such as the health or life of a student being threatened, but this will be only to the 'next of kin' name supplied by your child when they register.

Institutional procedures

Although you are not able to discuss your child's personal circumstances, you are able to discuss institutional procedures with staff. This can be useful to you if you want to find out what happens, in general, to students who fail their first year exams or do not meet deadlines for assignments. However, you will not be able to discuss specific circumstances unless your child has given consent.

UNDERSTANDING THE FREEDOM OF INFORMATION ACT

The Freedom of Information Act 2000 came into force on 1 January 2005. This Act gives people a general right of access to information held by or on behalf of public authorities.

This Act means that, although you can't receive personal information about your child, you can request information about committee structures, term dates, rules, regulations and procedures, research and so on. The learning provider has 20 days in which to respond to your request.

However, learning providers do not have to respond to all your requests. In certain circumstances data protection, confidentiality and commercial interests may exempt the information from being processed.

All learning providers should clearly state their policy on freedom of information and should provide a contact with whom you can get in touch.

Keeping in touch

Many colleges and universities understand that parents want to keep in touch with what is happening at the institution while their children are studying. Some now do this through a regular newsletter to parents, either via email or through the post. Consult the institution website or prospectus for information about how to register your details and receive the newsletter.

USEFUL INFORMATION

Useful addresses

The Basic Skills Agency is the national development agency for literacy, numeracy and related basic skills in England and Wales. The agency defines basic skills as 'the ability to read, write and speak English and use mathematics at a level necessary to function and progress at work and in society in general.' If your child is worried about their basic skills they can contact the agency for advice and information:

Basic Skills Agency

7th floor

Commonwealth House

1–19 New Oxford Street

London WC1A 1NU

Tel: 020 7405 4017

Website: www.basic-skills.co.uk

If you want to find out more about the Freedom of Information Act, or you are unhappy with the outcome of your request for information, you can contact the Information Commissioner at the address below:

The Information Commissioner

Wycliffe House

Water Lane

Wilmslow

Cheshire SJ9 5AF

Useful websites

www.informationcommissioner.gov.uk

More information about the Data Protection Act and the Freedom of Information Act can be obtained from this website.

Useful publications

If you are interested in finding out more about the Freedom of Information Act and the Data Protection Act, you may find the following books useful:

Brooke, H. (2004) *Your Right to Know: How to use the Freedom of Information Act and other access laws.* Pluto Press Ltd.

Rowe, H. (1999) *Data Protection Act 1998: A practical guide.* Tolley Publishing.

12

Understanding Student Life

If parents themselves haven't been away to college or university, they report being a little mystified about student life. Some say that their perceptions are influenced by the portrayal of students by the media. Often this is a negative portrayal with the problems of alcohol and debt taking precedence over the positive aspects of student life, as the following quotation illustrates:

> Before my son went to university I kept reading about drunken students and residents getting up in arms about them living in their area. I saw pictures of students throwing up and men flashing their bums and women showing their breasts. It scared me half to death. I know my son's sensible but I had visions of him getting in with the wrong crowd. Actually this was completely wrong and he worked very hard indeed.
>
> Sally

Researchers at Buckinghamshire Chilterns University College have recently conducted some research with 'first generation' undergraduates. These are students whose parents have not been away to university. They found that these students felt that their parents, although supportive morally and financially, could not be expected to know what they were going through. In particular, they felt that parents did not understand the importance of their social life.

This chapter provides information about student life, firstly to dispel some of the myths and secondly, to help you understand what your child will be going through during their time at college or university. It includes information on entertainment and social activities, sports and leisure, working in paid employment, volunteering, community activities and taking a gap year.

KNOWING ABOUT ENTERTAINMENT AND SOCIAL ACTIVITIES

Entertainment and social activities provided at colleges and universities vary enormously between institutions. Some campus universities, especially if they are run on a collegiate system, may have more bars and entertainment venues on campus than universities and colleges situated in city centres.

The following list provides an example of the types of entertainment that might be offered by your child's chosen college or university:

◆ comedy acts
◆ poetry readings
◆ film presentations
◆ alcoholic drink promotions and two for one discount
◆ happy hours
◆ karaoke nights
◆ fancy dress competitions
◆ seventies/eighties discos
◆ dance nights
◆ clubs on campus and transport to clubs off campus
◆ pub quizzes/trivial pursuit evenings
◆ formal dinners/balls
◆ bands/live music.

Colleges and universities employ their own security staff for events – some of these are full-time members of staff and others are students who are working part-time. All members of security staff receive training and know how to deal with the type of incidents that may arise.

Student ID cards need to be shown for most events and there are strict rules about the number of students allowed into the venue. Alcohol and drug abuse will not be tolerated and may lead to dismissal from the college or university.

UNDERSTANDING THE ACTIVITIES OF THE STUDENTS' UNION

Most colleges and universities will have a Students' Union, the size of which usually depends upon the size of the institution. Sabbatical officers are elected each year. These are usually final year students who stay on an extra year to take up their post and receive a wage. Non-sabbatical officers are also elected each year and take up their post while they continue with their studies.

Some of the larger Students' Unions employ a number of full-time members of staff in areas such as research and development, finance, catering and administration.

Students' Unions serve the interest of students in a variety of ways as the following list illustrates:

- running a student newspaper/radio station/television station
- running an advice and welfare service
- funding and organising a variety of clubs and societies

- organising student politics
- representing students' rights
- running a student shop
- arranging entertainment
- running bars and food outlets
- conducting research relevant to students
- arranging community volunteers.

The commercial role of the Students' Union

The Students' Union will probably be a member of NUS Services. This is the commercial arm of the Students' Union movement in the UK. It specialises in collective purchasing arrangements and direct marketing to reach the student population.

NUS Services enables companies to target the student market by providing a sampling pack distributed to all first year students each year. When your child joins the Students' Union they will receive a welcome pack containing a variety of free samples, vouchers, free gifts and information about local facilities. NUS Services also arranges promotions offering free newspapers, cheap stationery, and discounted food and drink.

Some individual Students' Unions organise special offers with local companies and provide a card or booklet containing vouchers and details of these offers. Through these arrangements your child can receive up to ten per cent discount on high street entertainment or in shops and bookstores off campus.

The political role of the Students' Union

The Students' Union exists to serve the needs of students. On an internal level this may be representing their rights at educational tribunals. For example, if your child feels they have been treated unfairly by their learning provider they can discuss their case with a trained person who will be able to decide whether they have a case to fight.

On an external level some of the more politically active Students' Unions may arrange activities such as organising coaches to national demonstrations or arranging for students to meet with their local MP.

The advice and welfare service will be able to help your child if they have any problems with issues such as accommodation, council tax, employment law or income tax.

Student representatives liaise between course tutors and students, making sure that courses meet the requirements of students and helping to overcome any problems that may arise. Your child can stand for election as a course representative if they wish.

KNOWING ABOUT SPORTS AND LEISURE FACILITIES

The number of sports and leisure facilities available will depend upon which university or college your child decides to attend. Some universities have a reputation for excelling in sports and they may provide more sports facilities than other universities.

The following list provides an example of the types of sport and leisure activities your child might be offered by their college or university. Teams may be available for both women and men:

- football
- hockey
- netball/basketball
- rugby
- cricket
- volleyball
- pool/billiards/snooker
- swimming
- racquet sports – squash/badminton/tennis
- water-sports – rowing/sailing/canoeing/windsurfing/ scuba diving
- golf
- athletics
- climbing/mountaineering/hill-walking/orienteering
- table tennis
- fencing
- aerobics/keep fit
- yoga/Tai chi/meditation/Pilates.

If your child excels at a particular sport and wishes to compete against other students, they should find out which institution has a reputation for excelling at that sport. These universities may have more and better facilities available which may be free of charge if your child is committed to their training. Also, scholarships might be available (see Chapter 5).

Paying for sports and leisure facilities

Most universities and colleges will make a charge for sports and leisure facilities. However, your child may find that they are able to make use of certain facilities, such as football pitches and running tracks, free of charge.

Prices vary enormously between institutions. Most universities operate a sports card system. For an annual payment your child is able to purchase a card that entitles them to use the sporting facilities for a reduced payment or free of charge. The price of this card varies between institutions, but is usually in the region of £35–£55 a year.

Some institutions will offer discounts to students who book sports facilities on a regular basis. If your child decides to join a sports club they will have to pay a membership fee but may receive discounts or free sporting facilities.

KNOWING ABOUT STUDENT EMPLOYMENT

Research by the National Union of Students suggests that over 90 per cent of UK based students work in paid employment during the vacations, with between 40–70 per cent working in paid employment at some time during the term-time. For some students this need to work is due to financial necessity, whereas for others it is to gain valuable work experience.

Over half of all employed students obtain jobs on campus. The following jobs are commonly available on university and college campuses throughout the UK:

- bar work
- glass collectors
- waitresses/waiters
- cooks/chefs

- dishwashers
- administrators
- mentors
- note-takers
- research assistants
- cleaners
- tour guides
- demonstrators
- lab assistants
- receptionists
- security personnel.

If your child decides to obtain a job on campus, they will find that there are several advantages:

- They can work in close proximity to where they live and study.

- Their employers will be used to working with students and should be flexible and understanding if study pressures become too great or they have to take time off for examinations.

- They will be employed with fellow students and can make lasting friendships.

- They can meet other students whilst working.

- They can gain valuable work experience in a safe and supportive environment.

- They can earn extra money, often on a flexible basis.

Popular jobs for students off campus tend to be in offices, pubs, cafés or restaurants. A major growth area in many parts of the country is in telesales and working for call centres. Many students are finding work in this sector as the working hours are flexible with plenty of evening and weekend work available. Also, for those who are good at what they do, incentives and bonus schemes can mean that wages are increased considerably.

College and university employment regulations

The amount of hours your child decides to work is usually their own decision and will depend upon how much time they can spare and how much money they want or need to earn.

However, some colleges and universities have regulations about the number of hours a week a student is able to spend in paid employment during term-time. These limits are provided in an attempt to make sure that employment does not distract students from their studies. If your child is thinking of obtaining paid employment, they must find out whether the university or college has such regulations.

Student employment services

To meet the demand for student employment, universities and colleges throughout the country have set up their own employment services. Some are run by Students' Unions, some by university careers services and some by personnel departments of the university.

Advisers in the employment services liaise with employers in the local area and advertise opportunities in their offices, via a newsletter and/or email to individual registered students. The employment services are not agencies – your child will have to liaise with each prospective employer, apply for the job and be paid by the employer.

Many employment services have made an agreement which means that, as a student, your child can access the services of another college or university to find employment. This is useful if they come home for the vacation and want to find part-time work.

KNOWING ABOUT VOLUNTARY WORK OPPORTUNITIES

Most of the larger colleges and universities have an organisation or department which arranges voluntary activities for students. This organisation might be managed by students, the Students' Union or by the careers service and may use a variety of names such as Community Action, Student Volunteers, Community Link or Volunteer Office.

There are a wide variety of opportunities available if your child decides to undertake voluntary work when they are a student. Opportunities to volunteer are available in the following areas:

◆ animals
◆ art and culture
◆ children
◆ disability
◆ education/literacy
◆ elderly
◆ environment/conservation
◆ health care/hospitals/caring professions
◆ human rights

- legal aid and justice
- mental health
- mentoring
- museums
- outdoor activities
- prisoners/young offenders
- psychology
- sports activities
- teaching
- women's groups.

Gaining qualifications through voluntary work

There are a variety of schemes available for students who wish to gain qualifications or awards through the voluntary work they undertake. Four of these schemes are listed below.

- **The Management Skills Award (InsightPlus)** – this scheme, endorsed by the Institute of Leadership and Management, is available for students in both paid and voluntary work. It offers nationally recognised accreditation for management skills acquired outside the academic curriculum and is available for students in sixth forms, colleges and universities. For more information consult www.insightplus.co.uk.

- **Millennium Volunteers** – through this scheme, when a student has completed 100 hours of volunteering they are presented with an Award signed by the Minister for Skills and Vocational Education. When the target of 200 hours volunteering is reached, they receive an Award of Excellence signed by the Secretary of State. The scheme is available for young people aged 16–24.

For more information consult www.millenniumvolunteers.gov.uk.

♦ **The Duke of Edinburgh Award** – this is available for young people aged 14–17 and for people aged 18–25. Students can choose from a huge range of volunteering activities in this country and abroad. For more information consult www.theaward.org.

♦ **Academic credits** – some universities will offer the opportunity to gain credits for the voluntary work that students do if it is relevant to their course. If your child is interested in this they should speak to their tutor.

TAKING A GAP YEAR

Some students find that they are not ready to enter college or university straight after leaving school or college. This may be because they feel they need a break from studying, or it may be because they feel they want to experience more of life and work before they continue with their studies. These students decide to defer entry for a year. This is called taking a 'gap year'.

There are many opportunities available if your child wishes to take a gap year. These include:

♦ becoming a volunteer in the UK or overseas
♦ participating in an expedition
♦ taking part in a cultural exchange
♦ working in the UK or overseas
♦ learning a language/studying for a TEFL (Teching English as a Foreign Language qualification).

If your child decides to take a gap year, and uses it wisely, you will find that they gain valuable work experience which will be of use to their future career and life in general.

They may also grow in confidence and mature as a person, gaining valuable life experiences that they will treasure, sometimes for the rest of their life. Students find it a fulfilling and worthwhile experience, often taking the opportunity to travel to other countries and work with different cultures.

USEFUL INFORMATION

Useful addresses

More information about student entertainment, sports, leisure and employment can be obtained from the National Union of Students:

The National Union of Students (NUS)

461 Holloway Road

London N7 6LJ

Website: www.nusonline.co.uk

Further details about the Duke of Edinburgh Award can be obtained from:

The Duke of Edinburgh's Award

Gulliver House

Madeira Walk

Windsor

Berkshire SL4 1EU

Tel: 01753 727400

Email: theawardinbusiness@theaward.org

Useful websites

www.nases.org.uk

This is the website of the National Association of Student Employment

Services (NASES). On this site your child can find an alphabetical list of student employment services in colleges and universities throughout the country. Leaflets covering issues such as applying for jobs, income tax and national insurance are available on this site.

www.tiger.gov.uk.
For more information about employment rights and the national minimum wage, consult Tiger (Tailored Interactive Guidance on Employment Rights). This website is designed to provide a user-friendly guide through employment law.

www.yearoutgroup.org
This website offers advice and guidance on choosing a suitable gap year programme and information is available for young people, their parents and advisers. It includes useful guidelines on asking the right questions when your child makes their choices and what needs organising before they go on their placement.

www.gapyearjobs.co.uk
Through this website your child can access details of jobs around the world that may be suitable for their gap year.

www.gap.org.uk
GAP Activity Projects provide volunteering opportunities overseas for 17–19 year old volunteers.

www.travellersworldwide.com
Through this organisation your child can find voluntary work placements overseas.

Useful publications

Worldwide Volunteering (4th edition) published by How To Books is a useful directory of volunteer projects for young people.

If your child is thinking about taking a gap year, they might find the following books useful:

Hecht, S. (2004) *The Gap Year Guidebook 2004/05*. John Catt Educational Ltd.

Butcher, V. (2003) *Taking a Year Off*. Trotman.

Griffith, S. (2003) *Taking a Gap Year*. Vacation Work Publications.

Vandome, N. (2005) *Planning Your Gap Year*. How To Books.

13

Helping Them to Keep Safe and Secure

In my research, it was found that another of the main concerns that parents have about their children going away to college or university is to do with their child's safety, as Julie points out:

> It is worrying 'cos it's the first time she's really been away from home, you know? I do worry about her, walking home at night, going out with friends, doing all the things students do, but then I 'spose you've got to let them go sometime.
>
> Julie, 51

A Home Office survey found that one-third of the students who took part in their research had been victims of crime in 2002. Of these, 12 per cent were the victims of theft or attempted theft and ten per cent were the victim of burglary. Other crimes included stalking, harassment and violence.

These problems can occur in all areas of society, but as a student your child may be more vulnerable. This is because they might move to a new area with which they are unfamiliar. They may not know which parts of the city are unsafe and which areas to avoid.

If they rent privately, the accommodation may not be as secure as your home, or they might be on a strict budget which means they have to rent accommodation in a rougher part of town.

However, although your child may not have too much control over their budget, or where they live, there are many steps they can take to reduce the chance of crime. This chapter discusses the ways in which you can help your child to keep safe and secure while they are studying.

SECURITY IN HALLS OF RESIDENCE

The Home Office survey found that nearly 12 per cent of students in private rented accommodation had experienced a burglary, compared with five per cent of students who lived in university accommodation.

Most colleges and universities recommend that first year students, especially those who are moving away from their home town, live in halls of residence for their first year. This provides more safety and security than your child might receive in private rented accommodation.

Halls have locks to outside doors and locks to each study bedroom. Many have spy holes in the doors. Some have security officers patrolling the grounds 24 hours a day and wardens living in the halls. The wardens are trained in health, safety and security issues – they will be able to help your child if they encounter any problems.

All security staff and wardens can be accessed through the university switchboard and halls will contain internal telephones for students to use.

However, even with all these security measures in place, theft does occur from rooms and it is recommended that your child take out insurance to cover any loss. Some universities now arrange insurance for students living in halls of residence and this cost may be covered in the rent.

CHOOSING SECURE HALLS OF RESIDENCE

If your child chooses to live in halls of residence in their first year it will give them a chance to familiarise themselves with the town and local area. If they then decide to move into private rented accommodation they will know the popular student areas and the areas to avoid.

When you go to view accommodation with your child ask questions about security and the availability of security staff and wardens. Try to speak to other students and ask them if they have ever encountered any problems. If the accommodation is on the ground floor or first floor, are measures in place to stop people gaining access?

Also your child will need to think about vacations – would their property be safe being left in the accommodation? Is there the possibility of secure storage?

Some colleges and universities have a busy conference schedule through the vacations and let student bedrooms to delegates. Will your child need to remove their property from halls if the room is to be let for conferences? Does their insurance cover their property left over the vacation?

CHOOSING SECURE PRIVATE RENTED ACCOMMODATION

If your child prefers to live in private rented accommodation you should start looking early as this increases your chances of finding something suitable. Popular houses in student areas tend to be snapped up quickly, so you may need to start looking as early as January before your child starts their course.

Your child should speak to staff in the accommodation office before making their choices. If they use accommodation recommended by the university, you know that it meets certain approved standards. Your child should also find out whether there are any areas that have more trouble than others. Is it recommended that students stay away from certain areas?

Viewing checklist

When viewing accommodation, your child should consider the following points:

♦ Do the locks look secure?

♦ Are there security bolts and chains?

♦ Are window locks in place?

♦ Are there any tell-tale signs of recent break-ins such as replacement glass, cracked door frames and forced windows? Look for the same in neighbouring properties.

♦ Are the boundaries to the property complete and secure? Would it be possible for somebody to climb over them easily?

♦ Is there public right of way near the property, such as alleyways or footpaths, which could pose a threat?

◆ Is the property overlooked by other properties which could provide extra security?

When your child moves into a property, they should make sure that expensive equipment cannot be viewed through the window.

INCREASING AWARENESS OF PERSONAL SAFETY

As a parent you will have been encouraging your child to think about personal safety throughout their lives. However, if your child is about to move away from home for the first time and become an independent person, they need to think a little more about issues of personal safety.

Avoiding crime against the person

Students can speak to staff in their Students' Union to find out whether there are any places they should avoid. Many Students' Unions give free attack alarms to their students. Your child should take up this offer and always carry the alarm with them.

Students should never walk alone at night. If they want to walk home from a night out, they should do so in a group. If they are on their own, they should call a taxi. Some colleges and universities have an agreement with the local taxi firm that enables students who have run out of money to be taken home and pay at a later date.

Students should always be aware of who is behind them, even in the daytime. They should make sure that people do not follow them into halls of residence (without the use of a key).

Most muggings and assaults happen outside pubs and clubs between 10pm and 6am. Students should be encouraged to think before they go out and drink alcohol. Do they know how they are going to get home? They need to think also about their friends and shouldn't let anyone leave by themselves.

Relationships with local people

Some local people resent students and the student way of life. Your child should avoid conflict and never get into an argument with local people, especially when everyone has been drinking.

When out in large groups all students should be encouraged to be aware of others around them – they must take care not to aggravate people by being loud and annoying.

It is important that students consider local residents when returning from a night out and if they are having parties late at night. Universities will not tolerate continual noise and disturbances and this could result in expulsion from university-owned property.

Avoiding theft and burglaries

Cash machines should be used wisely – everyone should check for tampering and make sure there is not someone behind them who could read their number. Money should be put away safely while at the machine and the card hidden.

Your child should be encouraged to not take out more money than they need and keep cards and chequebooks in a separate place in their accommodation.

All card numbers and mobile telephone details should be noted so that if anything does get stolen they can be cancelled immediately. Your child should make sure that they alert the authorities as soon as they are aware of the loss.

You should encourage your child to think about any valuable items they may have – is it really necessary to take them to college? If it is, they should mark their property with the initials of their college or university and their student ID number. They can use an ultraviolet pen to do this – many Students' Unions give them away free. The marking is invisible under normal light and won't damage their property.

They should always lock their house and/or room, even if just going out for a short time. Windows should not be left open when they are not in the room. Keys should not be left where they can be taken and should be kept away from windows and doors.

COPING WITH CRIME

If your child sees signs of a break-in to their property, they should not go in alone. Instead they should go to a friend or neighbour's house and call the police.

All crime should be reported immediately to the police – the Home Office survey found that 60 per cent of all incidents were not reported. This leaves assailants free to find another victim.

The police can put victims of crime in touch with victim support groups. University counselling and medical services are available for students – many will offer 24 hour cover for students who need advice and support.

INCREASING AWARENESS OF FIRE SAFETY

Each year there are over 70,000 house fires in the UK. If your child chooses to live in multiple-occupancy, private rented accommodation there is a higher chance that they could have a fire than if they are living in the family home. However, through careful organisation and planning, and by behaving responsibly, they can reduce the risks.

Fire safety in halls of residence

All buildings have the potential to catch fire, especially multiple occupancy buildings. However, all halls of residence have to pass stringent tests – they must contain the right number of fire doors and escapes, they will need to display and test evacuation procedures and test all electrical equipment on a regular basis.

If your child decides to live in halls of residence they should become familiar with the evacuation procedures and make sure they take part in all fire alarm tests.

All halls of residence will have strict rules about what can be used in study bedrooms. Some of these rules are because of fire safety and they should not be broken. This may include restrictions on the use of candles, plug adaptors and electrical appliances in the room. Many halls of residence now have a no smoking policy.

If your child has invited guests into their hall, they must make sure that their guests are familiar with evacuation procedures. Many halls will request that guests are signed in and out as a safety precaution and they will request that students inform the warden if they are going to be away from their room for more than 24 hours.

Fire safety in private rented accommodation

When you view accommodation with your child, ask the landlord whether the property has been inspected by the council to ensure safe and secure student housing.

Working with the fire brigade and the police, council inspectors will check gas appliances, electrical equipment and smoke alarms to make sure that they are all in good and safe working order. They will also check that rooms have close-fitting doors and that there is an adequate escape route in place. These checks not only cover fire safety, but also cover security, energy efficiency and amenities.

When your child moves into the accommodation they should be encouraged to discuss fire safety with other members of the household. They should make a fire action plan so that everyone knows how to get out of the house if there is a fire. The escape route should be kept free from clutter and the keys kept in a place where they can be found easily.

Acting responsibly

All housemates should be encouraged to act responsibly and make sure they adhere to the following:

◆ Take care when cooking with hot oil and never leave cooking unattended – 59 per cent of fires in the home are cooking related.

♦ Never leave candles unattended and always make sure they are placed in a heat resistant holder that won't fall over. Candles must be extinguished when leaving the room. University halls of residence ban the use of candles because they are so dangerous.

♦ If anybody in the house smokes they must make sure they always extinguish their cigarettes. They should always use a proper ash tray and not be tempted to stub out cigarettes in anything that could catch fire. They should not empty recently used ash trays into a bin.

♦ Students should not smoke in bed and they should take extra care if they have been drinking alcohol – half of all deaths from domestic fires happen between 10pm and 8am.

♦ Students must not place clothes on portable or gas heaters to dry, or close enough to fall on to a fire.

♦ Electrical sockets should not be overloaded or one adaptor plugged into another.

♦ Electrical appliances should be turned off at the wall when not in use.

COPING WITH FIRE

If your child discovers a fire in their property, they should try to alert everyone in the building by shouting 'fire' loudly and banging on bedroom doors as they evacuate. If they are in halls, they should break the nearest alarm and vacate the building. They must not stop to collect belongings or return into the building for any reason.

The fire brigade should be alerted immediately – do not assume others have made the call. The advice given by the fire brigade is **GET OUT – STAY OUT – CALL 999**.

Your child should speak to their accommodation officer for more information. Many will provide an accommodation hunting checklist which includes questions to ask about fire safety.

REMAINING SAFE ON FIELD TRIPS

If field trips are a part of your child's course extra health and safety precautions are required. At most colleges and universities your child will be required to sign a safety registration form on which they include all personal details and contact numbers in case of emergencies.

Some colleges and universities will require them to watch a safety video or read a safety leaflet/manual before they attend the field trip. Once on the field trip your child will need to follow these instructions:

- Obey all safety instructions given by the course leader or instructor. Failure to obey instructions can lead to dismissal from the trip. As the field trip course-work may be assessed, this will have an adverse influence on course marks.

- Stay with the group unless clear consent has been given to work alone.

- Wear appropriate clothing for the type of weather and terrain – seek advice before the trip commences (see Chapter 10).

◆ Inform the leader or tutor of any medical condition relevant to the field trip. Guidance can be obtained from the *student health service* or doctor on campus.

◆ Observe the country code when in rural areas.

USEFUL INFORMATION

Useful websites

www.nusonline.co.uk

Advice on student accommodation, personal and fire safety and all other aspects of student life can be obtained from this website.

www.victimsupport.org.uk

If your child becomes a victim of crime, Victim Support is a national charity offering a free and confidential service. More details can be obtained from their website.

www.secureyourmotor.gov.uk

More information about how to keep your child's car, motorbike or scooter secure can be obtained from this website.

www.firekills.gov.uk

General information about fire safety can be obtained from this website.

www.upmystreet.co.uk

Before choosing accommodation, your child can consult this website to find out how the area performs on crime and policing.

14

Helping Them to Keep Healthy and Happy

As a parent you will naturally want your child to remain healthy and happy while they are studying. Parents in my research felt that this was an anxious time, especially for those with independent children, as Alex illustrates:

> How do you know how they're getting on? How do you know they're OK? My son's never been one for communicating with his parents – he's very independent. I want to make sure he's all right but I don't want to seem overbearing – that drives him crazy.
>
> Alex

Despite Alex's concerns, it is possible to help your child to prepare for their studies and life away from home without appearing over-bearing.

This chapter offers advice on helping your child to remain healthy and happy while they are studying at college or university. It discusses their working environment, maintaining health and motivation, coping with the pressures of study, raising awareness of drugs and alcohol and knowing where to go for help and advice.

CREATING A HEALTHY WORKING ENVIRONMENT

It is important for students to have a healthy working

environment as this will help them to be comfortable in their studies and should help them to remain motivated.

If possible your child should use their working environment only for studying and for important paper work. This could be a desk in a study bedroom or an office in the family home.

Items that are used for leisure, such as televisions or radios, should be kept away from their working space. They need to be able to make a clear distinction between work and leisure time and if they have a separate working space they will find this much easier.

It is important also to make sure that the furniture is suitable – well designed furniture can reduce pain and injury, increase productivity, and improve mood and morale. Good furniture can also help to eliminate awkward posture.

Living at home

If your child intends to live with you while they are studying, you need to create a working environment that will help, rather than hinder, their studies. This means that you need to have furniture and equipment that is comfortable and suits your child's style of working, and they will need to find a quiet space free from distractions.

Your child will need to set ground rules – the rest of the family should acknowledge that quiet time is needed and that important work is not disturbed. This may mean that your family will have to decide who can and who can't use computing equipment.

Living in halls of residence

If your child intends to live in halls of residence, they should check that the study bedroom is adequate for their needs. All study bedrooms will contain a desk and chair and should have suitable ventilation and lighting. Your child can supply other equipment to make their working environment more comfortable.

Living in private rented accommodation

If your child chooses private rented accommodation that has been advertised to students, there should be a private place to study in the bedroom. This should, at the very least, include a suitable chair and desk. When you and your child look around private accommodation, check that there is a suitable place to study in the room.

Your child should try the chair and desk and check whether there is adequate ventilation and light in the room. They should also think about noise levels and check that there is nothing outside the window that could distract them from their studies.

Housemates should be chosen carefully – it is important that everyone in the house has the same attitude towards respecting privacy and quiet time.

Choosing furniture

If you and your child have the luxury of choosing furniture, you should try to adhere as much as possible to the health and safety guidelines listed below:

◆ The chair should be at a height that allows a 90° angle at the elbows for typing.

- The sitting position should be with thighs horizontal, lower legs vertical and feet flat on the floor or on a footrest.

- The seat should swivel and have a padded, curved seat that does not cut into the back of the knees.

- The back of the chair should offer firm support and the sitting position should be upright with the back on the lumbar support.

- There should be plenty of leg room.

- The desk needs to be big enough to allow for all computing equipment and provide space for paperwork.

- Frequently used items should be kept within easy reach.

- The top of the computer screen should be at eye level or slightly lower.

- The viewing distance of the screen should be 18–24 inches.

- The screen should be free of glare, shadows and reflections.

- The mouse should be placed level with the keyboard and near enough so that stretching is not required.

- There should be enough light – natural daylight is best, but for working in the evenings there should be good lighting that does not produce glare or shadows on books, paper or screen.

- The room should have good, natural ventilation.

MAINTAINING PERSONAL HEALTH

As a parent you will be anxious to make sure that your child maintains their health while they are studying. In addition to being very worrying for you, poor health can stop your child attending lectures and seminars and it will lower their motivation to work independently. Everyday tasks become harder and more stressful and social relationships might suffer.

If they have not done so recently, your child should get their eyesight and hearing checked before they go to college as poor eyesight and hearing can have a detrimental affect on their studies.

As an adult you know that three of the most important aspects of maintaining health and well-being are diet, exercise and sleep. You can help your child to prepare for college by addressing these issues in advance.

Diet

If this is your child's first time away from home they may not be an experienced cook. However, maintaining a good diet is essential. If your child intends to live in private rented accommodation or non-catered halls it is important that they learn to cook as this is the best way to use fresh, healthy ingredients and control what they are eating, as Joan points out:

> My daughter spent seven years in further education... One of the most important things a parent can do is to teach their child to cook food which is cheap, nutritious and quick without being junk food. Homemade pasta meals, baked potatoes, fresh vegetables etc keep them well fed and healthy.
>
> Joan

Before your child goes to college give them some cooking lessons and tips. At first, keep cooking simple. Encourage them to follow recipes that are uncomplicated – some useful cookbooks are listed at the end of this chapter. They should also be encouraged to limit fat and salt, avoid junk food and eat plenty of fresh fruit and vegetables.

If your child is eating in catered halls or canteens, they should try to vary what they eat, again making sure that they limit their fat and salt intake. Colleges and universities are striving to make their meals healthy and may offer a variety of differently priced meal packages for their students.

Exercise

Your child should try to exercise as much as possible. Colleges and universities have a wide variety of sports and leisure facilities and some of these are free of charge (see Chapter 12). Plenty of exercise will help your child to sleep and a fit body helps to create a fit mind.

Exercise should be taken between study sessions – it is important for your child to move their limbs frequently and avoid marathon study sessions as these can be counter-productive, both mentally and physically.

Sleep

Your child needs to set a good sleeping pattern and try not to let student life disrupt this pattern too much. They need to limit the number of late nights and get plenty of sleep. They should avoid stimulants, such as alcohol, coffee and nicotine, before they go to bed.

HELPING YOUR CHILD TO REMAIN MOTIVATED

Everybody experiences dips in their motivation levels at some time in their lives. It is natural and nothing to be concerned about. However, where your child's studies are concerned, there are a few tips you can take note of to help keep their motivation levels high:

◆ Make sure they choose a subject in which they have a high level of interest. Don't force them to study something that doesn't interest them because you think it will be good for their future careers.

◆ Encourage them to think about their learning style and choose a course and institution that will not clash with this style. There are several 'learning style' question-naires on the internet that they can fill in to help them think about these issues.

◆ Before they begin their course, discuss their reasons for going to college or university. These might include personal fulfilment, better employment prospects and so on. Refer back to this discussion during times of low motivation.

◆ Encourage them to set clear aims and objectives. What do they hope to achieve from the course? How do they intend to meet their goals?

◆ Encourage them to make use of available help at their college or university, such as student support groups, counsellors and study support.

◆ Try not to put undue pressure on your child. Students can face a lot of pressure and stress when studying. As a parent, you know the importance of offering support and guidance, rather than aggravating the situation. Look out for the signs of stress and suggest ways of reducing the problems.

◆ If your child is living at home while they are studying, make sure they have a quiet, suitable environment in which to study. Make sure other family members respect their study time and study materials, including computing equipment.

◆ Financial concerns can cause worry and stress which helps to aggravate problems with personal motivation. You need to help your child overcome these problems, not necessarily by providing cash, but by helping them to understand the importance of money management and careful budgeting.

COPING WITH THE PRESSURES OF STUDY

As a student your child will be required to complete a certain amount of work at the required level each year of the course. Many students meet their course demands without feeling too much pressure. Indeed, a certain amount of pressure can be a good thing – it makes us work harder and produce better results.

However, a minority of students may find that, at some stage of their course, they are encountering too much pressure which leads to stress and anxiety. This may lead to difficulty coping with course requirements. It is important to be aware of personal stress as it is easier to deal with the problems as soon as they occur and before they escalate.

Dealing with stress

Some students find that stressful situations can have an adverse influence on their studies. If you believe your child is suffering from stress they should be encouraged to take action.

Some of the symptoms of stress are listed below. However, these symptoms can be due to other medical conditions and your child should always consult a doctor if they are concerned.

◆ skin rashes
◆ stomach pains
◆ muscle tension
◆ mood swings
◆ tiredness
◆ increased anxiety
◆ headaches
◆ increased irritability
◆ lack of concentration
◆ poor work and marks
◆ change in sleep patterns
◆ lack of motivation
◆ over- or under-eating
◆ increased dependency on drugs or alcohol.

If you think your child is suffering from stress, the following points may help:

◆ They should be encouraged to talk about problems and anxieties with family, friends and/or tutors. At most institutions students are allocated a personal tutor who is available to help with study and pastoral support.

Also, some institutions allocate student mentors to first year students to help with any problems they may encounter.

♦ It is important to escape from worries for a while – they should take a break if at all possible and use vacations wisely to relax and stop worrying about studies.

♦ Physical activity is useful to help people overcome anger and frustration, and relaxation techniques such as yoga and meditation help to calm the body and mind. Many universities run this type of course for students.

♦ Don't place extra pressure on your child by having unreasonable expectations. Your child does not have to be a perfectionist all the time. Consistent high marks are not the be all and end all of their course.

♦ Do not criticise your child.

♦ Encourage your child to avoid competition and cultivate co-operation instead. Gaining support from other students will help with their studies and their personal life. They should not fret about getting lower marks than someone else on the course.

RAISING AWARENESS OF DRUGS AND ALCOHOL

In my research with parents one of the worries they have about their children going away to college or university is that they are going to be exposed to the influence of alcohol and drugs, as Pete points out:

I know what it was like at college, I've been there and done that and read the book. I know he'll experiment, but I hope he'll be sensible. What worries me is if it all starts to get out of control. You hear so much about alcohol and drug problems these days.

Pete, 46

Students who live away from home do have greater freedom, but this does not mean that they are going to go off the rails. Most know the difference between right or wrong, good or bad.

They may experiment with things they haven't tried before, but most will know where to draw the line. Also, most students realise the importance of doing well on their course and know that drugs and alcohol will have a detrimental effect on their studies.

Alcohol and drug information, support and guidance

It is difficult for you to protect your child while they are away. However, there are members of staff at the college or university who have your child's best interests at heart. Welfare staff offer advice about drugs, counsellors offer support for those who need help. Sensible, down-to-earth information leaflets and guidance are provided by the Students' Union.

Your child will be provided with well-researched, unbiased information which will help them to think about the issues involved, so that they can make up their own minds and make the right choices.

Many colleges and universities now produce websites containing information about student health and well-being. These include information and advice on drugs and alcohol. Some also have a health visitor who will provide information and arrange presentations for new students.

Alcohol and drug policies

All colleges and universities have policies on alcohol and drug misuse amongst students and staff. These vary, but in general include the following:

◆ Anyone caught *supplying* illegal drugs will be reported to the police and asked to withdraw from the college or university.

◆ *Possession* of illegal drugs may be referred to the police and the student suspended until the outcome of the police prosecution is known.

◆ Misuse of drugs or alcohol that leads to nuisance or disruptive behaviour will lead to dismissal from university-owned accommodation and/or to a ban of recreational and social areas at the college or university.

◆ A student will not receive special concessions if they fail their course due to alcohol or drug misuse.

◆ If a course involves clinical placements or any other interaction with members of the public, and a student is found to be misusing drugs or alcohol, they will be required to leave the course.

FINDING PROFESSIONAL HELP AND SUPPORT

There are a variety of professional people working for colleges and universities who are available to help students when they encounter problems. These include medical personnel, welfare staff, counsellors and religious services.

Registering with a doctor

Most learning providers will have a *student health service* or *medical centre* on campus or they will be able to recommend a local doctor. Your child should be encouraged to register with a doctor as soon as they arrive. To do this they will need their medical card.

Doctors are trained in dealing with the types of health problems faced by students. Appointments with doctors and nurses can be arranged on campus and an emergency number is provided for evenings and weekends.

The *student health service* or *medical centre* will provide advice and information on issues such as contraception, sexual health, drug and alcohol abuse, stopping smoking, healthy eating and avoiding eating disorders. They will also provide vaccinations, immunisation and information for illnesses such as meningitis and mumps.

Some universities have their own dentist or will be able to recommend a local dentist for their students.

Using welfare services

Many college and university Students' Unions run an advice and welfare service for their members. Most places will have a trained, permanent member of staff who can offer help and advice on any welfare issue. Some of these services will have a 'drop-in' session and others will offer an appointment service. The facilities are free to students.

Using counselling services

Many universities and larger colleges employ their own student counsellor, and if they don't the welfare services will be able recommend a counsellor outside the college or university.

Student counsellors specialise in dealing with the problems faced by students and some are available 24 hours a day, seven days a week. A counsellor's role is to offer support and understanding and to listen and respond in a non-judgemental, non-critical way. University counselling services are free to students requesting counselling.

Using religious services

Many universities and larger colleges have their own chaplain and religious advisers. These may represent various faiths including Anglican, Roman Catholic, Methodist, Pentecostal, Buddhist, Hindu, Islam, Jewish and Sikh. Some will hold full-time appointments on campus whereas others are part-time, having congregations elsewhere and welcoming students into their communities.

Some colleges and universities invite in leaders of other denominations and/or provide prayer rooms for religious reflection and support. Most universities and some larger colleges have religious groups of various denominations set up by the students to offer services, social activities, comfort and support.

USEFUL INFORMATION

Useful addresses

The Health and Safety Executive produces free leaflets about working safely with computers and VDUs. More information can be obtained from:

Health and Safety Executive

Magdalen House

Trinity Road

Bootle

Merseyside L20 9QZ

Website: www.hse.gov.uk

Parents Against Drug Abuse (PADA) offers help and support for the parents and families of drug users. On their website you can find information about drugs – how they are used, the side effects, street names and spotting symptoms of drug misuse.

PADA

14 Church Parade

Ellesmere Port

South Wirral L65 2ER

Helpline: 08457 023 867

Website: www.btinternet.com/~padahelp

Useful websites

www.safety.ngfl.gov.uk

The DfES Superhighway Safety site provides comprehensive information and advice on all aspects of using ICT safely, including computer workstations and the internet. It also includes information on the Data Protection Act, firewalls, viruses, hacking and advice specifically for parents.

www.studenthealth.co.uk.
Consult this site for information on all aspects of student health. The information on the site is provided by doctors and updated weekly.

www.leeds.ac.uk/ahead4health.
The University of Leeds has produced a website for all students who may be suffering from mental health problems. It provides descriptions of problems, methods of coping and two self-help workbooks on problem solving and assertiveness.

www.drugeducationforum.co.uk
The Drug Education Forum is part of the National Children's Bureau and works to achieve the provision of effective drug education for all children and young people in England. There is a section for parents on this site.

Useful publications

The following books provide interesting and simple recipes for students who are new to cooking:

Clarke, C. (2002) The *Essential Student Cookbook: 400 budget recipes to leave home with.* Headline.
Clarke, C. (1999) *More Grub on Less Grant.* Headline.
Crook, S. (1998) T*he Survival Guide to Cooking in the Student Kitchen.* Foulsham.

(15)

Letting Go of Your Child

In my research some parents said that it was difficult to let their children go, especially when this would be the first time they have lived away from home. Parents wanted to help as much as possible, but knew that they would have to let their children fend for themselves, as Barbara illustrates:

> They're your children aren't they? You've loved and nurtured them all this time and suddenly they're ready to fly the nest. It's quite hard not having them around the place and it's even harder trying not to worry about them. It's a big leap going away like that and we wanted to do as much as we could to help, but I guess it's all about letting go and letting them get on with it really.
>
> Barbara, 37

It can be difficult for parents to strike the right balance. An important aspect of going away to college or university is that students become independent and learn how to cope with life. However, students can face many pressures, and it is only natural that as a parent you are concerned about their well-being.

This chapter describes the areas in which students need to develop their independence, such as managing their money, but also provides information about how you can help your child without appearing to be interfering or over-protective.

ENCOURAGING FINANCIAL INDEPENDENCE

Becoming financially independent is an important part of growing up. Some students find it quite a shock to go away to college or university and suddenly have to survive on quite small amounts of money.

In my research parents said that one of the most important ways to prepare their child for life away from home was to encourage financial independence. Not only does this help the transition from home to college to run smoothly, but it also saves valuable time once your child has begun their studies.

Also, if they have made certain preparations, such as opening a bank account and preparing a budget, they will find that payments of financial support that may be due to them are not delayed.

Opening a bank account

Most students will need to open a bank account when they begin their studies. This is because all financial support will be paid by cheque or direct into their bank account through the Bank Automated Clearing System (BACS). This includes student loans and any grants or sponsorship your child may receive.

Bank accounts are useful for setting up direct debits or standing orders to pay bills, loans and rent, and some employers prefer to make salary payments direct to bank accounts. Opening a bank account will also ensure that your child does not have to keep large amounts of cash on their person or in their room.

Your child should open a bank account as soon as possible before the course begins. That way, they can supply all the relevant details to the Student Loans Company in good time. However, your child should find out which banks are conveniently located in their intended place of study.

Choosing a bank

Banks work hard to attract student customers and offer a number of incentives. Although your child might be tempted by these incentives, they should be encouraged to think about the more practical aspects of opening a bank account:

- Does the bank offer a free overdraft facility? Many students find that they go overdrawn when they are studying.

- Does the bank offer free banking? Most banks will offer free banking on current accounts if your child stays in credit and some offer free banking on overdrafts as long as they stay within the agreed limit.

- How often will the bank send statements? It is useful to receive statements monthly so that your child can budget effectively.

- Does the bank have a wide network of cash machines available, especially near the university and near your home? Is it possible to access the cash machines of other banks free of charge?

- Does the account provide a cheque book, cheque card and switch/debit card?

♦ Does the account enable the use of telephone and online banking? If so, your child would be able to keep up-to-date with their account from their own PC 24 hours a day.

Using student advisers

Many banks, especially those that have branches on or near campus, have resident student advisers. Your child can arrange an appointment to discuss the available services.

Once they have opened a bank account they can arrange another meeting with the adviser to discuss all aspects of their money management. Often these people are graduates themselves and will have some useful advice to give.

ENCOURAGING CAREFUL MONEY MANAGEMENT

In my research some parents felt that their children were already quite wise about money matters. However, these parents felt that teaching their children about money management before they went away was still important as this would help to reduce financial problems while their children were studying.

Knowing the facts

If your child intends to continue with their education after compulsory schooling, they must realise that it can be expensive. The Barclay's Annual Graduate Survey found that 183,000 students who graduated from university in 2004 owed a total of £2.46 billion. This works out at an average of £13,501 owed per student.

If current trends continue, Barclays predicts that a student beginning their studies in 2005 will graduate owing almost £20,000.

However, through careful preparation and money management your child can keep down these costs and reduce the amount of money owed when they graduate.

If your child thinks about their budget before they go away to university, they will be better prepared to deal with the financial cost of student life. The types of expenditure your child can expect are discussed in Chapter 6. Sources of income are discussed in Chapters 4 and 5. Once your child knows what income and expenditure to expect, they can go on to plan their budget.

Planning the student budget

There are four simple stages to planning the student budget:

- keep all records of income and expenditure
- calculate income
- calculate expenditure
- work out the difference between the two.

If the difference between the two is positive, your child has the luxury of putting some money aside for when their studies become more expensive. If the difference between the two is negative, your child needs to think about how they can increase their income and reduce their expenditure.

Below is a sample budget planner which your child can use to help them with their budgeting.

SAMPLE BUDGET PLANNER

Course costs	Weekly expenditure
Tuition fees	
Books	
Photocopying	
Laser printing	
Stationery	
Sub-total	

Living costs	Weekly expenditure
Rent	
Gas	
Electricity	
Water rates	
Telephone	
Insurance	
Laundry	
Transport/travel	
Leisure and entertainment	
Food and drink	
Clothing	
Household goods	
TV licence	
Credit commitments	
Sports and hobbies	
Miscellaneous expenditure	
Sub-total	

Sources of income	Weekly income
Student loan	
Contribution from parents	
Sponsorship	
Employment	
Income from savings	
Benefits	
Other loans/grants	
Miscellaneous income	
Sub-total	
Total weekly profit/loss (larger figure minus smaller figure)	

DEALING WITH DEBT

Debt is defined as the use of unauthorised money which is left unpaid. Under this definition a student loan does not count as debt if it is paid back in accordance with the agreement.

However, any other money that is owed and left unpaid, such as library fines, accommodation fees and utility bills, is classed as debt. Getting into debt can cause problems for your child. If your child owes money to the college or university they may not be able to graduate. If they owe money to utility companies they may have their supply cut off or could receive a visit from the bailiffs.

The most common types of student debt are:

◆ unpaid utility bills
◆ unpaid rent
◆ unpaid council tax
◆ unauthorised overdraft
◆ unpaid library fines/fees
◆ missed payments on tuition fee instalments
◆ missed payments on hire purchase agreements
◆ missed payments on credit cards/store cards.

If your child learns how to keep records and plan their budget carefully they should avoid getting into debt. They should be encouraged to avoid credit as much as possible and not take out a credit card or store card or be tempted by a bank loan.

Many students find that it is useful to work in paid employment during the first and second years, building up spare cash to see them through their third year when study commitments might be greater. They should also exhaust all forms of student support, including student loans and hardship funds.

If your child finds themselves falling into debt they should seek advice immediately. Advice and welfare staff or student services will be able to offer advice about other sources of income.

ENCOURAGING INDEPENDENT LIVING

Every family is different – your child may already be very independent, or they may still rely heavily on you for tasks such as cooking, cleaning and laundry. How do you decide how much you should continue to do for your child when they begin their studies?

The first thing you need to do is talk to each other – what are their expectations? What can you do to make the transition easier for them? Is there anything specific they would like you to do, or would they like to fend for themselves? If this is the case, don't take anything personally. Your child understands the importance of independent living and it is you who has helped them to become mature enough to know that this is the case.

Also, remember that your child will be away for a number of years. The situation can easily change and you need to think about being prepared to go along with what your child needs if they ask for your help and if it aids their studies.

Deciding how much to help

In some research with second year university students living away from home I asked what were the most important things parents had done to help them in their first year. These items are listed below, with those being mentioned the most appearing at the top of the list:

- Provided small amounts of money when I most needed it.
- Bought me a computer.
- Welcomed me home during vacations and helped transport my possessions.
- Provided food parcels/supplied me with basics after vacations.
- Helped me buy books and course materials.
- Took me shopping in the vacations for essentials.
- Let me take some of my washing home.
- Always at the end of the telephone when I wanted a chat.
- Fed me well in the vacations.
- Taught me how to cook/bought recipe books.
- Helped stock my room.

As you can see from this list, most items are related to finance, food or comfort! The students were pleased that parents helped them financially and supported their studies by helping to provide computers, books and course materials.

Students were happy that parents were always there if they needed them and that they kept their rooms clean and comfortable for their return over vacations. Some students pointed out that their term-time accommodation wasn't so good and it made them appreciate the comforts of their parents' house when they went home.

Trying not to interfere

The same students were asked to list things their parents had done which they had not appreciated. These are listed below, with those mentioned the most often appearing at the top:

- Pressured me to work too hard.
- Tried to get me to study something I didn't want to study.
- Put too much pressure on me during exams.
- Worried and fretted that I was going to become a drug/alcohol addict.
- Wouldn't give me any cash and said I had to stand on my own two feet.
- Told me not to bring my washing home.
- Criticised my clothes/bought me clothes I would never wear.
- Didn't like my girlfriend/boyfriend.

As you can see from this list, the type of interference students didn't like relates to course choices, study pressures, lifestyle choices and finance.

Making generalisations from research results can be difficult. Your situation may be very different and your child's personality may be very different from the students interviewed in my research. However, these lists may be a good starting point for your discussion with your child about how much help and how little interference they want from their parents.

USEFUL INFORMATION

Useful addresses

The National Debtline is a national telephone helpline for people with debt problems in England, Wales and Scotland. The service is free, confidential and independent. Specialist advice is given over the telephone and backed up with free written self-help materials. If your child finds themselves in debt they can ring the free telephone number, consult the website or use the address below:

National Debtline
The Arch
48–52 Floodgate Street
Birmingham B5 5SL
Freephone: 0800 808 4000 (Mon–Fri 9am–9pm, Sat 9.30am–1pm)
Website: www.nationaldebtline.co.uk

Useful websites

www.support4learning.org.uk
This website contains a regularly updated summary of student bank accounts.

www.nusonline.co.uk
The National Union of Students provides estimates of average living costs for undergraduate students during one year of full-time study. These estimates are useful as a guide and will give you an idea of what you can expect to spend throughout your child's course.

Useful publications

Financial Survival for Students is another of my books. It covers all these issues in much greater depth, discussing sources of income and expenditure, and highlighting the importance of money management. Details of the book can be obtained from www.studentcash.org.uk.

Your child may find the following book useful:

Thomas, G. (2004) *Student Money Matters*, 2004. Trotman.

16

Understanding the Value of Education

Continuing into further and higher education is not just about gaining more qualifications to obtain a well-paid job. It is a whole life experience. You will find that your child matures and develops in many different ways – some will be expected and obvious, others will be unexpected and may not appear so obvious, as Jenny, a final year student, points out:

> I got involved in Community Action, helping disabled kids. Then I did some volunteering abroad one summer. Then some mates and I went travelling the next summer. It was all valuable experience and I never would have had the chance if I'd not gone to university. I intend to get a good job working for a charity and travelling abroad. I've now got some experience, but more importantly I think I've grown as a person and developed my skills. I didn't really know it was happening but when I fill in applications, I realise what I've done.
>
> Jenny, 21

This chapter highlights the benefits to be gained by continuing in education after compulsory schooling. It includes issues of personal development and fulfilment, increases in knowledge and intellect, increase in choices, and better employment and salaries prospects.

INCREASING SELF-CONFIDENCE AND ESTEEM

Over the years I have conducted many focus groups with students who have completed their studies in further and higher education. When they discuss the personal benefits they have gained, one of the most important benefits is seen to be an increase in personal confidence and a rise in self-esteem.

When the students in the focus groups were asked how further and higher education had helped to increase their confidence, they mentioned the following:

- ◆ Mixing and socialising with new people from the UK and overseas. Some people are from similar backgrounds, some from very different backgrounds. Students develop confidence in speaking to people and making new friends throughout their course.

- ◆ Developing thoughts and arguments in lectures, seminars and tutorials. At first it is daunting, especially if students are a little unconfident. However, over the course confidence increases and students are able to put across their views much better and in a variety of different situations.

- ◆ Living independently. Students have to learn to live on their own – look after themselves, cook, clean clothes and manage finances. This brings them into contact with many different people and organisations. Their confidence develops as their independence grows.

- ◆ Passing exams and assignments. Students said that one of the best ways to increase confidence and self-esteem was to pass their exams and receive good marks for their assignments. Graduation day was mentioned over and over again as a great day for self-esteem!

INCREASING CHOICES

My research has shown that people who have higher levels of confidence and self-esteem believe that they have more choices available in life. They tend to be more confident in trying new jobs and putting themselves forward for promotion and requesting higher salaries.

Due to high levels of confidence these people tend to be more successful, often getting what they want. This is because people perceive them to be confident 'go-getters' who will be an asset in the workforce.

People with higher qualifications are able to consider more employment options, as Adam noted when he finished his studies:

> Suddenly the country became much bigger. All of a sudden many more jobs were open to me. I could look at jobs in all the broadsheets and in the technical journals, as well as local jobs. It was incredible how much more choice there was.
>
> Adam, 23

INCREASING SATISFACTION

Raising confidence and self-esteem is not all about succeeding in the world of employment. It is also about feeling satisfied, fulfilled and happy with life. People with higher levels of confidence and self-esteem tend to travel more often, socialise to a greater degree and have more stable relationships.

In my research with adults who had returned to education later in life, they said that gaining a degree had enabled them to feel more satisfied and fulfilled with life. It was as if they had achieved some type of balance that had not previously been present, as Barry points out:

> Doing a degree was the best move I ever made. Before I had felt this niggling thing – it's hard to describe, perhaps restless, perhaps not quite happy, perhaps not all there, if you know what I mean. When I'd done my degree I sort of became more balanced, more satisfied and obviously happier. Things don't get to me so much now and I seem to know where I'm going.
>
> Barry, 32

INCREASING KNOWLEDGE AND INTELLECT

Another important benefit to be gained from continuing with their education, students felt, is an increase in their personal knowledge and intellectual capacity. If your child chooses their course and institution carefully, and they complete all the work requested of them, it will almost certainly increase their knowledge and intellect.

This has many practical advantages which help graduates with their social and working lives, as Isobel points out:

> I learnt so much on my course and I can apply it to everyday living and to my work. It's good to know why people might behave in a certain way or why my work colleagues might be scared of change. It helps you to understand people and to empathise with them.
>
> Isobel, 23

BUILDING TRANSFERABLE SKILLS

Transferable skills are all those skills that your child develops while they are away at college or university that can be transferred easily to the world of work. Employers are keen to see that they have developed, and are aware of, such skills.

A recent Open University project found that employers were looking for students with confidence, initiative and an ability to reflect on what they are doing, in addition to technical skills and academic knowledge.

It is probable that your child will develop some or all of the following skills while they are studying:

- organisation skills
- time-management
- the ability to reflect
- skills of analysis, evaluation and synthesis
- the ability to review and critique
- communication skills – verbal and written
- team-working skills
- the ability to work independently, using their initiative
- the ability to meet deadlines
- social skills
- IT skills
- reading skills
- research skills
- listening skills
- the ability to work under pressure
- the ability to empathise.

INCREASING EMPLOYMENT PROSPECTS

The Organisation for Economic Co-operation and Development (OECD) published the results of a survey in September 2004, which found that graduates in OECD countries are more likely to find a job than non-graduates. For women, 78 per cent with a degree are in employment, compared with 63 per cent of women without a degree. For men, 89 per cent with a degree are in employment, compared with 84 per cent of men without a degree.

These statistics show that continuing into higher education significantly enhances your child's employment prospects. It also enhances their career choices, opening up a larger selection of possible careers.

The government predicts that 50 per cent of jobs in the UK economy between 2000 and 2012 will be graduate posts. These predictions were made in August 2004 and are an amendment of figures published in the Government White Paper on Higher Education which suggested that 80 per cent up to 2010 would require a degree.

Although the figures are disputed by some people including the Conservative Party, most agree that employment opportunities are greatly enhanced for those obtaining a degree. Employers want graduates working for them because they are seen to be people who are confident, can communicate effectively and are able to reflect on what they are doing and consider ways to improve their work.

Most universities keep records of their graduates' first employment destinations after they have finished their course. You will find these figures contained in university prospectuses or on websites.

INCREASING SALARY POTENTIAL

Figures from Graduate Prospects suggest that salaries for university leavers in the summer of 2005 will range from £13,242 to £36,000. It is expected that one in four graduates will receive a salary of more than £25,000.

The OECD survey mentioned above found that, in the UK, graduates earn 59 per cent more than non-graduates. Also, in the UK, a person who enters higher education after leaving school can expect to gain 10 per cnt on their investment every year from graduation to the age of 65. This compares with those who don't enter higher education receiving a rate of return of four per cent a year.

Interestingly, the researchers found that eliminating tuition fees as an incentive to increasing participation is of limited value, adding just 1.8 per cent on average to the return on a degree.

These statistics show that the potential for earning higher salaries increases significantly as your child continues into further and higher education.

USEFUL INFORMATION

Useful websites

www.prospects.ac.uk

This is the official graduate careers website and is a useful place to find out what type of skills employers are seeking.

www.nases.org.uk

This website contains more information about developing skills relevant to employment, and information about applying for jobs, income tax and national insurance.

www.work-experience.org

This is the official website of the National Council for Work Experience. It provides more information about work experience and work-related learning for students.

www.studentzone.org.uk

This website offers links to organisations offering advice on many aspects of student employment and careers.

www.morethanwork.net

This website helps students to identify their skills, build a successful CV, understand their employment rights and find contact details for their local job shop.

Glossary of Terms

Basic skills The Basic Skills Agency (BSA) defines basic skills as the ability to read, write and speak in English and use mathematics at a level necessary to function and progress at work and society in general. Research by the BSA suggests that around one in six people may have a low level of competence in basic skills. Colleges and universities will provide extra help for students who struggle with basic skills.

Board of Examiners This is a group of university academics who make decisions on a student's progress at the end of the academic year and on final degree classifications.

Clearing System This is a system operated by the Universities and Colleges Admissions Service (UCAS) which enables students to identify and apply for places on courses that still have vacancies, after the publication of A Levels and other equivalent results.

Continual assessment On some courses, rather than have an examination at the end, a student's progress is continually assessed. This means that, at various stages throughout the course, they have to complete an assessed piece of work. This might be a written assignment, a presentation or some other type of project.

Course A course is an ordered sequence of teaching or learning over a period of time. It is governed by regulations or requirements that may be imposed by an examining body or a learning provider. The length of a course may vary from a few hours to several years. Students may be required to attend a course at an institution or they can study on a course by distance learning, correspondence or flexible learning.

Credit accumulation and transfer Upon successful completion of modules your child will acquire credits. Many learning providers have entered into an agreement whereby students can build up these credits and transfer them between courses and institutions. When enough credits have been built up, the final qualification can be obtained.

Credits can be built up when studying in Europe through the European Credit Transfer System. Some students choose to study only one module abroad, whereas others might choose to study a variety of modules over the full academic year.

Deferral If your child has been unable to complete part of an assessment due to illness or other reasons, and where there is written evidence to support this, the board of examiners may allow your child to defer some of that assessment until a later date.

Also, if your child has been offered a place at university but decides to take a year out from their studies, they can request a deferral until the following year. Universities will review all requests for a deferral, but a positive decision is not guaranteed.

Dissertation A dissertation is an extended project and report (usually around 10,000 words) that is carried out towards the end of a degree course. In your child's final year of a degree course they will choose a relevant subject, undertake the research and analysis and complete the work by writing a report.

Distance learning This is a course of study where a student does not attend classes at a particular institution, but instead interacts with a tutor via post, telephone, email or fax. This type of course may be known as a correspondence course, flexible learning or e-learning.

Examination An examination is a formal test or assessment to test knowledge, understanding, skill and/or competence. Examinations may be written, oral, aural, practical tests or a combination of the above. If your child has taken their GCSEs and A Levels they will know about examination procedures.

Extenuating circumstances These are circumstances beyond your child's control which would cause them to perform less well in coursework or examinations than they might have otherwise been expected to do, and which will affect them for a significant amount of time. If written evidence is provided these circumstances will be taken into account when the board of examiners makes it decision.

External examiner This is an academic appointed from another university. Their role is to ensure that examinations are conducted and marked fairly. They have the right to see and moderate all work submitted for a degree.

Field trip A field trip involves outside visits to a place or organisation that can help to clarify what is being taught.

Group-work Students may be required to work in groups on a particular project or piece of work. Sometimes this may be assessed and may count towards their final marks.

Independent research As your child progresses with their studies, they will be required to conduct independent research. There are two types of research – primary research and secondary research.

Key skills In education key skills tend to refer to the skills students will need to help them to be successful in whatever they intend to do in later life. These may include communication skills, numeracy, the use of information technology and learning how to learn.

Learning outcomes A learning outcome is what a student will know, understand, or be able to do on completion of a course. All course information packages should define clearly the learning outcomes – your child needs to make sure that these match their goals. If there is a mismatch, your child should consider whether there is a more suitable course available.

Learning styles We all learn in different ways and some of us may adapt the way we learn to suit the situation. Researchers have attempted to describe the different ways we learn and these are called learning styles. We are more comfortable when we are being taught in a way that suits our learning style.

Lecture This is formal tuition given by a lecturer to a large number of students. This often takes place in a lecture theatre and, in most cases, lasts for one to two hours. Students are required to listen and take notes.

Module/modularisation Many courses now run on a modular basis. This means that students study a number of modules that make up their course. Each module is assessed separately and credits can be built up towards the final qualification. Some students may study full-time, working on several modules, whereas others may study part-time, perhaps only studying one module at a time.

Many learning providers have entered into an agreement whereby students can build up credits and transfer them between courses and institutions. When enough credits have been built up, the final qualification can be obtained. It is possible to study abroad and gain credits through the European Credit Transfer System.

National Qualifications Framework This is the system of qualifications used in England. There are eight levels from entry to degrees and professional qualifications. The framework includes qualifications such as GCSEs, NVQs and BTECs.

Referral If your child fails a module, the board of examiners may permit them to retake or re-sit parts of the assessment for that module.

Semester Many colleges and universities, instead of having the traditional three terms, operate on a semester system. Typically there are two semesters in the academic year, although some universities retain the three-term system.

Seminar This is a small group discussion on a particular topic. Often students are required to present seminars themselves.

Tutorial This is a small group or individual session led by a tutor to discuss a specific topic. This type of teaching method tends to be utilised more by some universities than others and is used more often during postgraduate study.

Tutor feedback When your child hands in any work to their tutor, they will mark the work and write comments on the assignment. This feedback will help your child to improve their work as the course progresses. Some tutors will offer face-to-face feedback if they feel it will be of benefit.

Viva voce **examinations** These are oral examinations used in universities. They tend to be used in science subjects to test a student's knowledge of a project, or for postgraduate qualifications such as a PhD.

Useful Addresses

GOVERNMENT DEPARTMENTS

Department for Education and Science
Sanctuary Buildings
Great Smith Street
London SW1P 3BT
Tel: 0870 000 2288
Website: www.dfes.gov.uk

Department for Employment and Learning
Student Finance Branch
Room 407
Adelaide House
39–49 Adelaide Street
Belfast BT2 8FD
Tel: 028 9025 7728
Website: www.delni.gov.uk

The Information Commissioner
Wycliffe House
Water Lane
Wilmslow
Cheshire SJ9 5AF

QUALIFICATIONS IN THE UK

The Qualifications and Curriculum Authority
83 Piccadilly

London W1J 8QA
Tel: 020 7509 5555
Email: info@qca.org.uk

The Scottish Qualifications Authority
24 Douglas Street
Glasgow G2 7NQ
Tel: 0845 279 1000
Email: customer@sqa.org.uk

The Qualifications, Curriculum and Assessment Authority for Wales
Castle Buildings
Womanby Street
Cardiff CF10 1SX
Tel: 029 2037 5400
Email: info@accac.org.uk

Council for the Curriculum, Examinations and Assessment
29 Clarendon Road
Clarendon Dock
Belfast BT1 3BG
Tel: 028 9026 1200
Email: info@ccea.org.uk

FURTHER EDUCATION INFORMATION
Learning and Skills Council (Head Office)
101 Lockhurst Lane
Foleshill
Coventry CV6 5RS
General enquiries: 0870 9006 800

Fax: 02476 703 314
Email: info@lsc.gov.uk

HIGHER EDUCATION FUNDING
Student Loans Company Limited
100 Bothwell Street
Glasgow G2 7JD
Tel: 0800 405 010
Website: www.slc.co.uk

The Student Awards Agency for Scotland
3 Redheughs Rigg
South Gyle
Edinburgh EH12 9YT
Tel: 0131 476 8212
Website: www.saas.gov.uk.

OVERSEAS STUDY
ERASMUS
R&D Building
University of Kent
Canterbury
Kent CT2 7PD
Tel: 01227 762712
Fax: 01227 762711
Email: info@erasmus.ac.uk
Website: www.erasmus.ac.uk

GOVERNMENT PUBLICATIONS
DfES Publications
PO Box 5050
Sherwood Park

Annesley
Nottingham NG15 0DJ
Tel: 0845 60 222 60
Email: dfes@prolog.uk.com

The Stationery Office
PO Box 29
St Crispin's House
Duke Street
Norwich NR3 1GN
Tel: 0870 600 5522
Email: customer.services@tso.co.uk
Website: www.tso.co.uk/bookshop

SOCIAL WORK COURSE INFORMATION AND FUNDING

Care Council for Wales
6th Floor
South Gate House
Wood Street
Cardiff CF10 1EW
Tel: 029 2022 6257
Email: info@ccwales.org.uk
Website: www.ccwales.org.uk

Scottish Social Services Council
Compass House
11 Riverside Drive
Dundee DD1 4NY
Tel: 0845 60 30 891
Email: enquiries@sssc.uk.com
Website: www.sssc.uk.com.

Social Services Inspectorate
C4
Castle Buildings
Stormont
Tel: 028 9052 0517
Email: dorothy.vance@dhsspsni.gov.uk
Website: www.dhsspsni.gov.uk

General Social Care Council
Goldings House
2 Hay's Lane
London SE1 2HB
Tel: 020 7397 5835
Email: bursaries@gscc.org.uk
Website: www.gscc.org.uk

TRUSTS AND CHARITIES
Educational Grants Advisory Service (EGAS)
501-505 Kingsland Road
Dalston
London E8 4AU
Information line: 020 7254 6251

Uniaid Foundation
The Tower Building
12th Floor
11 York Road
London SE1 7NX
Tel: 020 7922 1699
Website: www.uniaid.org.uk

National Debtline
The Arch
48–52 Floodgate Street
Birmingham B5 5SL
Freephone: 0800 808 4000 (Mon–Fri 9am–9pm, Sat 9.30am–1pm)
Website: www.nationaldebtline.co.uk

NHS FUNDING AND COURSE INFORMATION
NHS Student Grants Unit
22 Plymouth Road
Blackpool FY3 7JS
Tel: 01253 655 655
Website: www.nhspa.gov.uk

NHS Wales Student Awards Unit
2nd Floor
Golate House
101 St Mary's Street
Cardiff CF10 1DX
Tel: 029 2026 1495

Department of Health
PO Box 777
London SE1 6XH
Tel: 08701 555 455
Website: www.doh.gov.uk

DANCE AND DRAMA COURSE INFORMATION AND FUNDING
Council for Dance Education and Training (CDET)
Toynbee Hall

28 Commercial Street
London E1 6LS
Answers for Dancers information line: 0901 800 0014
Email: info@cdet.org.uk
Website: www.cdet.org.uk

National Council for Drama Training
1–7 Woburn Walk
London WC1H 0JJ
Tel: 020 7387 3650
Email: info@ncdt.co.uk
Website: www.ncdt.co.uk

STUDENT INFORMATION
National Union of Students
461 Holloway Road
London N7 6LJ
Tel: 020 7272 8900
Website: www.nusonline.co.uk

STUDENTS WITH DISABILITIES
Student Finance Delivery Division
2F – Area C
Mowden Hall
Staindrop Road
Darlington DL3 9BG
Tel: 01325 392822
Website: www.dfes.gov.uk/studentsupport

Adult Dyslexic Organisation
336 Brixton Road
London SW9 7AA

Tel: 020 7924 9559

Royal National Institute of the Blind
105 Judd Street
London WC1H 9NE
Helpline: 0845 766 9999
Fax: 020 7388 2034
Website: www.rnib.org.uk/student

Royal National Institute for Deaf People
19–23 Featherstone Street
London EC1Y 8SL
Tel: 020 7296 8000
Fax: 020 7296 8199
Textphone: 020 7296 8001
Freephone voicephone: 0808 8080123
Freephone textphone: 0808 8089000
Website: www.rnid.org.uk

Skill: the National Bureau for Students with Disabilities
Chapter House
18–20 Crucifix Lane
London SE1 3JW
Tel: 0800 328 5050
Minicom: 0800 068 2422
Website: www.skill.org.uk

BASIC SKILLS
Basic Skills Agency
7th Floor
Commonwealth House
1–19 New Oxford Street

London WC1A 1NU
Tel: 020 7405 4017
Website: www.basic-skills.co.uk

HEALTH AND SAFETY

Health and Safety Executive
Magdalen House
Trinity Road
Bootle
Merseyside L20 9QZ
Website: www.hse.gov.uk

Index